People, Performance, and Succeeding as a Manager

HBR Work Smart Series

Rise faster with quick reads,
real stories, and expert advice.

It's not easy to navigate the world of work when you're exploring who you are and what you want in life. How do you translate your interests, skills, and education into building a career you love?

The **HBR Work Smart Series** features the topics that matter to you most in your early career, including being yourself at work, collaborating with (sometimes difficult) colleagues and bosses, managing your mental health, and weighing major job decisions. Each title includes chapter recaps and links to video, audio, and more. The HBR Work Smart books are your practical guides to stepping into your professional life and moving forward with confidence.

Books in the series include:

Authenticity, Identity, and Being Yourself at Work

Bosses, Coworkers, and Building Great Work Relationships

Boundaries, Priorities, and Finding Work-Life Balance

Experience, Opportunity, and Developing Your Career

People, Performance, and Succeeding as a Manager

Writing, Presenting, and Communicating with Confidence

**WORK
SMART**

*Tips for Navigating
Your Career*

People, Performance, and **Succeeding as a Manager**

HARVARD BUSINESS
REVIEW PRESS
Boston, Massachusetts

Copyright 2025 Harvard Business School Publishing Corporation

All rights reserved

Printed in the United States of America

10 9 8 7 6 5 4 3 2 1

No part of this publication may be reproduced, stored in or introduced into a retrieval system, or transmitted, in any form, or by any means (electronic, mechanical, photocopying, recording, or otherwise), without the prior permission of the publisher. Requests for permission should be directed to permissions@harvardbusiness.org, or mailed to Permissions, Harvard Business School Publishing, 60 Harvard Way, Boston, Massachusetts 02163.

The web addresses referenced in this book were live and correct at the time of the book's publication but may be subject to change.

Cataloging-in-Publication data is forthcoming.

ISBN: 979-8-89279-006-2
eISBN: 979-8-89279-007-9

The paper used in this publication meets the requirements of the American National Standard for Permanence of Paper for Publications and Documents in Libraries and Archives Z39.48-1992.

CONTENTS

SECTION 3

Setting Team Norms

SECTION 4

Developing Your Employees

SECTION 5

Giving Feedback

SECTION 6

Managing Your Well-Being and Growth

So Now You're a Manager . . .

by Jennifer Dary

You've just emerged from a meeting with a new title: manager. Maybe you celebrate. Maybe you text someone. Perhaps you're thinking, "It's about time!" or "Holy crap, they picked me!" Maybe you feel that you've crested a career-path mountain, that you've earned that LinkedIn title update.

You should feel proud of yourself. Not everyone gets here. Also: buckle up. You're about to change.

The first time I was promoted to the role of manager, I had one direct report. I was friendly, she was friendly. She told me everything I wanted to hear in our weekly one-on-one meetings. She said she was happy with her job and satisfied with her growth. *But was she?*

Though I had excellent relationships with everyone else at the company, my direct report was the one person whose opinion I couldn't access. Her agreeable nature gave me one signal, but I couldn't tell if she thought I was an inspirational figure or a total jerk behind closed doors. I even asked a colleague on the leadership team to bring me any feedback he heard, positive or negative. I sensed that we needed to build more trust, but despite my best efforts, I had no control over how quickly that could happen.

Readjusting my efforts, I managed her on instinct. I focused on being reliable, continued to invite her feedback, kept an eye on the dynamics of our team and how others treated her. I shielded her when I could and made suggestions when it seemed appropriate. If I couldn't read her thoughts, I was going to act like the manager I'd want to have. So that's what I did until I left the company a year later. To this day, I don't know if I was ever offering her what she wanted from a manager.

Today, I leverage that experience by training new managers through my leadership coaching business. All of my clients want to be strong and supportive bosses, but they encounter obstacles along the way. There are many reasons attendees seek my training, but they usually come down to just a few that are simple and straightforward:

- They want to be good managers.

- They discover that the skills that got them promoted are not the skills they need for management.

- They feel anxious about conflict—with their team, former peers, and even their own bosses.

- Being a manager can be lonely.

Fortunately, there are ways to overcome these challenges.

What It Means to Be a Manager

Though you've likely observed many managers in action—both the good and the bad—you can't know what you don't know until you're in the role yourself. As a manager, you will be permitted into new circles, invited to different meetings, and given access to confidential information. Your presence bears new weight, and others will look to you to lead them.

While leaders don't always manage, managers always lead. Leading requires good listening skills, strong communication, and a compelling vision. On top of that, managers are responsible for specific individuals and teams, ensuring that they reach established expectations while growing their skill set at the same time. To succeed in this role, you need access to a nuanced tool set. Giving regular feedback, developing career plans, directing work pace and performance management, serving as a bridge between senior leadership and the team at large . . . when wielded expertly, all of these tools propel the team forward.

But what if you've been handed the tool belt with no accompanying training? When do you use a hammer, a wrench, or a chainsaw? That's what this book will teach you.

We start by looking at what it means to create a new managerial identity. You'll discover how to establish yourself in the role, even if you're younger or have less experience than the people you manage. You'll identify how to define your distinct work style. And you'll learn from a first-time, first-generation manager how to build a foundation of confidence in the role.

But management is an interactive job. Building trust must be a priority in your first few months. Section 2 explains how to encourage your team to be open with you (something I struggled with in my first managerial role) and helps you identify ways you may be eroding their trust. You'll leverage this trust when unveiling a new direction or delivering challenging news. Remember, management is not a popularity contest. In chapter 6, leadership coach Ramona Shaw encourages managers to prioritize being respected over being liked. Preach.

Section 3 will guide you through the nitty-gritty—establishing team norms and behaviors. How many meetings are too many? What purpose do one-on-ones serve? Are there guidelines for communication and conflict? The experts here help you navigate these areas so you're setting up your team for success right from the start.

With management responsibilities come other tall asks: How do you ensure your employees are growing, and how do you provide tough feedback? How do you encourage your top performers while managing someone who is struggling at work? And how do you let someone go? Sections 4 and 5 offer answers to these questions and more as they dive into the basics of development, feedback, and recognition.

As a manager, you'll serve a vast number of stakeholders, including your direct reports, the team, your own manager, the company and, depending on your industry, clients, customers, or other external groups. There may be moments where you feel like a 10-headed monster, flinging yourself through days of back-to-back meetings with not much to show for it. We end this book by reminding you to be kind with yourself: You can't lead anyone if you're burned out. Put your oxygen mask on first.

In time, you'll find ease in the role. You'll leave meetings victorious after delivering hard feedback. Your most reluctant report will open up in a one-on-one and share a priceless perspective on the team's future. You'll celebrate a big launch with your team and appreciate these now familiar coworkers. Tiny wins will accrue, and one day you'll feel like those issues you struggled with at the start are in the past, now that you have the right tools—and know how to use them.

Someone once said that people don't leave jobs, they leave managers. The flip side is true too; people will leave jobs to *follow* managers. Managers who are trustworthy, respected, and skilled will always find opportunities. Ultimately, good managers are one of the most valuable assets a company can have. Luckily for your employers and your people, they've got you.

Establishing Yourself as a Leader

When Your Employees Have More Experience Than You

by Jodi Glickman

Becoming a manager can feel intimidating. Suddenly, you're in charge of not only your success, but also the growth and achievements of your team.

And if you're in the early stages of your career, this transition can be even more difficult. You may still be trying to figure out who you are and what you want. And yet, it's now your responsibility to bring out the best in others and inspire them to do great work.

While there are plenty of challenges that come along with taking on a management position early in your career, among your first will probably be managing and leading people who have more years of experience than you. How do you engender their trust, respect, and admiration?

Check Your Insecurities

You may not have as many years of experience as some of your direct reports, but that doesn't mean you don't deserve your leadership position.

If you find yourself worrying about not being taken seriously or respected by your employees, take a step back. Try looking for real-world evidence that supports your thoughts. Then, look for evidence that suggests the opposite.

Ask yourself: Would I have been promoted into this role if my supervisor, and the company, thought I was incompetent? Probably not. You may also find that your colleagues don't actually attribute competence or high performance to years of experience.

No matter what you discover, remind yourself of this often: You belong in the seat you are occupying.

Get Everyone on the Same Page

People get picked to be managers because of their talents and people skills. This could be your ability to make sound decisions, bring different people together, influence others, and stay calm during tough moments.

When you start out, engage with your direct reports in one-on-ones. Talk about your vision and goals for the team. Remember that they come with experience, and their experience can help you refine your ideas. Leave space for two-way dialogue and stay open to feedback.

Be Confident Enough to Be Vulnerable

If you are feeling unsure or insecure while leading, your team will be able to read that energy and may become unsure of your leadership, too. That's why it's important to practice confidence when speaking to them: Make eye contact, use gestures to accentuate your point, stand or sit up straight, and maintain strong body language. Practicing your delivery method will help you speak with conviction, be clear about your intentions, and show up as the leader you aspire to be.

At the same time, don't be afraid to be vulnerable and relate to your team during challenging projects or conversations. You're not expected to walk in on day one and be an expert. You are, however, expected to be 100% honest—about the challenges your team is facing, the strategies you are contemplating, and your willingness to listen and learn from those around you.

When you share your ideas, leave room for your team to (honestly) reflect on them. Let them know that you value their opinions and experiences. You could say, "This is what I had in mind, and here's why. . . . What do you think? Do you agree? Disagree? Is there anything we're missing here? I'd love to have your thoughts and feedback."

Especially when it comes to more experienced direct reports who may have worked at the organization longer than you have, solicit their opinions on what has worked in the past, what their current working style is, and where things are due for change. Ask how you can best support them. Say, "I know we started this new workflow last month. I wanted to know how you feel about it and take some time to review it."

When you do that, be receptive to their ideas and views. Be transparent about your desire to establish a true partnership. Your goal should be to bring out the best in one another.

Be Generous

Leaders who are generous—with their time, energy, and resources, with sharing credit and giving meaningful feedback—are the ones who earn respect and admiration from their teams. Generosity at its most basic is this: Walking in every day and asking yourself, "How can I make my teams' lives better or easier?" "What can I do to help them do their jobs successfully?" "How can I be an advocate for their ideas or support their initiatives?" "How can I showcase what they do right and have their back when things go wrong?"

Recognize that your employees may be at a different life stage than you. Spend time to learn more about them. Get a deeper sense of any barriers they may be facing and how you can try to remove them or, at the very least, be creative in coming up with workarounds or ways to collaborate. For instance, you may find that one employee has to homeschool their child during work hours. What can you do to support them and make their lives a little easier?

Being empathetic is critical to being a good leader. Do your best to accommodate different needs.

. . .

Regardless of your years of experience, you have what it takes to be a successful manager and leader. Rely on your transferable skills, show strength and humility, and demonstrate your willingness to learn alongside your team.

QUICK RECAP

Becoming a manager comes with many challenges, including having to manage people with more experience than you. How do you move forward?

- **Check your insecurities.** Remind yourself of this often: You belong in the seat you are occupying.

- **Get everyone on the same page.** Talk to your direct reports about your vision and goals for the team and leave space for two-way dialogue.

- **Be confident enough to be vulnerable.** Practice confidence when speaking to your team, but don't be afraid to show vulnerability during challenging conversations.

- **Be generous.** Being empathetic is critical to being a good leader. Do your best to accommodate different needs.

Adapted from "When You're Younger Than the People You Manage," on hbr.org, December 24, 2020.

How can you ensure you'll be taken seriously as a manager?
Listen to this podcast:

2

How to Determine Your Work Style as a Manager

by Claire Hughes Johnson

When I was an executive at Google, I worked with a talented manager who had one big flaw: He told his team *everything*.

Eli (name has been changed to preserve anonymity) often broke company news to his team before anyone else had a chance to share it, or worried his team members by telling them how stressed he was about, say, a reorganization of our division. When I talked to him about it, Eli agreed that this was a problem. But he would not change his behavior.

Soon after one of these conversations, Eli and I took part in a training session in which we each reflected on the values that were most important to us. I'll never forget the story Eli told. When he was seven or eight, Eli's mom was diagnosed with breast cancer. Nobody told Eli what was happening—his family tried to pretend everything was OK. Eventually, Eli's mother was hospitalized, and he wasn't allowed to visit her. One day, Eli's stepfather picked him up from school and took him out to his favorite diner. Over pancakes, Eli learned his mother had died.

Eli's value was transparency.

Both Eli and I came away from that exercise changed. I learned that when you're dealing with a difficult behavior—in yourself or in others—there's often a deeper root cause. Eli gained a stronger awareness of why he communicated the way he did.

This episode underscored a core principle I've emphasized throughout my career: Self-awareness in the workplace is always a superpower, but when you're a manager, it's even more important. You need to understand your work style—your strengths and weaknesses—in order to do your best work and help other people do theirs.

Here, I'll share two exercises you can use to develop self-awareness and communicate your work style and values to your teams.

Identify Your Work Style

Throughout my career, and in studying many personality and work-style assessments, I've found that two main criteria often determine people's work styles: (1) whether they're more introverted or extroverted; and (2) whether they're more task-oriented or people-oriented.

To determine whether you're more introverted or extroverted, ask yourself:

- Do I talk to think or think to talk?

- Do I do my best work with others or by myself?

- Do meetings and group work make me feel more energized or depleted?

I don't consider myself a heavy extrovert, for example, but I do need to talk out my ideas to arrive at the best answers. If you're more extroverted, you may find that talking through a challenge with a colleague or collaboratively problem-solving with your team will help you come to a more thought-out conclusion. If you're more introverted, you may find it more productive to think through plans or solutions independently before sharing them with a wider group for feedback.

To determine whether you're more task-oriented or people-oriented, consider:

- Am I more likely to focus on the work itself or on the people doing it?

- Do I tend to place more value on doing things quickly and efficiently or on bringing people along in the process and generating consensus for the path forward?

- When faced with a problem, am I more likely to start thinking about solutions or gathering perspectives on the situation from others?

Task-oriented people tend to pay more attention to the most efficient way to get things done and less on generating buy-in around the right approach. Folks who are more people-oriented tend to build consensus around the path forward, but they may lose sight of completing the task efficiently in the interest of bringing people along.

FIGURE 2-1

What's your work style?

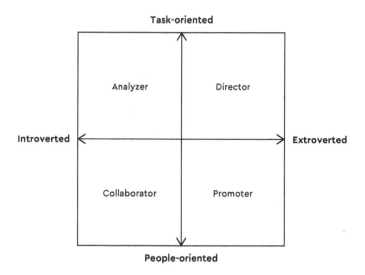

Source: Adapted from Claire Hughes Johnson, *Scaling People: Tactics for Management and Company Building* (San Francisco: Stripe Press, 2023).

Where you fall on the axes in figure 2-1 will help you determine which of four work styles you fall into. I call them the analyzer, the director, the collaborator, and the promoter.

- *Analyzers* make rigorous, deliberate, and data-driven decisions. They're great at coming to the right answer, but they may have trouble acting without data. They may not be as skilled at collaborating, building processes, or seeking consensus.

- *Directors* are opinionated and great at establishing a vision. They have a bias toward action because they care about getting to the right outcomes quickly, but that means they often dictate exactly what needs to be done, which can disempower others, or do the work themselves without bringing others along.

- *Collaborators* care a lot about stakeholders or customers, whether that's an internal customer (like another team) or an external one. They're great at building systems and processes, but they may overcomplicate those systems because they don't want to leave anyone out.

- *Promoters* tend to have a lot of ideas. They're great at building relationships, and they're able to articulate an inspiring narrative that others want to get behind. But they're less concerned with details or administration, so they're often great starters but not always finishers.

Knowing your work style—and, ideally, that of your direct reports—will help you be a more effective and empathetic manager. In terms of your team, you can use the work-style assessment to ensure it's well-rounded, representing a mix of work-style preferences and strengths. For yourself, it will help you be mindful of your weaker points and when they're likely to show up, allowing you to prepare a plan for how you'll address them.

For example, as a director, I know that when faced with a problem or an urgent situation, I tend to be too quick to jump to action. Instead, I try to follow this rule in team settings: Before diving into solutions, I ask a question first. This keeps me from moving too quickly and helps my team work on their own problem-solving skills.

Articulate Your Values

The next step is to identify the values that motivate you. The combination of your work style and values guides how you lead and collaborate with others. Try this exercise:

1. Imagine yourself late in life, reflecting on your career. In the end, what was most important to you?

2. Write down 10 values that represent your ideal of that fulfilled life. (Some examples might be accomplishment, balance, community, joy, impact, and learning.)

3. Narrow down the list to five values, then three.

4. Write down activities that embody each value. If your value is *excellence*, for example, an activity might be that you never deliver a project unless it's nearly perfect.

5. Consider the positive outcomes of those values as well as the trade-offs. Valuing excellence, for instance, might also mean you push your team to deliver great work, but often set unrealistic expectations or unattainable deadlines.

Think about the values you identified. How do they intersect with your work style? Recognizing this can help you uncover and address your unconscious biases, lean into your strengths, and better communicate both of them with others.

For example, if you value community and are a collaborator, you may go the extra mile to connect with and create psychological safety for your team. But perhaps through this exercise, you noticed that you don't give people enough autonomy. Or maybe you value impact and are a director. You may be excellent at driving results, but less experienced at slowing down and teaching your direct reports the skills they need to learn on their own.

Communicate Your Work Style and Values

Be open with your direct reports about your work style and the values that drive you so they can understand how best to work with you and provide feedback on the unconscious biases your values inevitably create. You can even create a "Working with Me" document that clearly outlines how you like to collaborate, your work style, your communication preferences, the areas you're working on, and more. Better yet, have your team members walk through the same exercise as a group, with a greater focus on their communication preferences and work habits. Then, adjust to meet each other in the middle and watch how quickly your collaboration improves.

The values exercise Eli and I did was a master class in self- and mutual awareness. It became clear that Eli wanted to communicate with his team in a more productive way, but withholding information felt like a betrayal of his commitment to transparency. Understanding this, we were able to find a path forward: Eli would consult his peers and manager before sharing critical decisions with his team, and he would be more measured in how he communicated those decisions. But we would also commit to trustworthy and clear communication as part of every plan we

made. He and his team were stronger for it, as was our entire
organization.

. . .

Self-awareness is a skill that will serve you throughout your
career, and one that you should continue to develop and nurture
over time. It can be the key trait that differentiates you from
others early on, and it will help you steer toward work that makes
the most of what you have to offer—now and in the years ahead
of you.

QUICK RECAP

It's important to understand your work style as a manager so
you can do your best work and help other people do theirs.

- Are you introverted or extroverted? More task-oriented or
  people-oriented? Depending on how you identify, you're
  either an analyzer, a director, a collaborator, or a promoter.

- What are the values that motivate you? The combination
  of your work style and values guides how you lead and collaborate with others.

- Once you've identified your work style and values, discuss
  them with your direct reports so they can understand how
  best to work with you.

Adapted from "How to Determine Your Work Style as a New Manager,"
on hbr.org, March 3, 2023.

Lessons from a First-Time, First-Generation Manager

by Kela Lester

One of the many lessons Black parents instill in their children is that in order to succeed, we have to be twice as good as our peers: twice as smart, twice as talented. This advice is ingrained in everything from literature to pop culture. Now, there's data to back it up: Despite being among the most educated and productive, Black workers and other workers from marginalized communities are overrepresented in low-wage, entry-level jobs and underrepresented in senior leadership and executive roles.[1]

While there's extensive research on the glass ceiling and how to break it, there's less talk about its close relative, the "concrete wall"—a set of obstacles that keep Black, Indigenous, and people of color (BIPOC) professionals, especially women, from securing high-level positions.

The concrete wall, as described by Ella L. J. Bell Smith, a professor of management sciences at the Tuck School of Business, "limits your capacity to learn and understand what's [happening] on the other side—the culture, the behavior, the expectations, the rules. If you don't know what's on the other side, and nobody's telling you what the rules are—or if somebody keeps changing the rules without your knowing it—you can't play the game."[2]

So, what happens when you finally chip away at the wall and move into a managerial position for the first time? What should you do if you're the first person in your family to navigate this new opportunity?

Here are three baseline lessons I've learned in my few years as a first-time and first-generation manager.

Start Within

Confidence is a cornerstone of leadership. Proposing a new idea? You need to display your expertise to get stakeholder buy-in. Hosting a meeting? People won't engage with you unless they aspire to be a part of something larger. Setting expectations and giving feedback? No one listens to someone who isn't sure of themselves. The list goes on.

Whenever you feel unsure of yourself as a new leader, take a moment to remember the unique upbringing and point of view that got you to where you are today. When I first began my role as a manager, I thought that the key to success was code-switching—changing my appearance, behavior, or speech to fit in with the majority group. It wasn't until I gained the confidence to share and celebrate my personality that I realized my power. Tapping into my resilience, adaptability, and resourcefulness successfully positioned me to contribute to company culture, confront racial bias, and break unrealistic expectations. Once I was comfortable being myself, I not only pursued opportunities that were right for the real me, but could also bring another perception to ideas that others overlooked.

Whatever your own story may be, use your strengths to build a foundation of confidence. Then, add to it. One way you can do this is by emulating the leadership styles of mentors or managers you admire. Observe them, ask for their advice, and take on the traits that resonate with you most. These may be emotional intelligence, humility, kindness, creativity, integrity, courage, and even the ability to persuade others, depending on your approach. Likewise, leave behind the traits that don't feel right, or that were more hurtful than helpful to you as a direct report.

Last, celebrate your wins. In my first leadership role, I tracked mine monthly in a draft email and pulled it up whenever I could use the extra pat on the back. The more you practice self-confidence in small ways, the more comfortable you'll become. If you want a unified team to venture with you into the unknown, it all starts from within.

Step Back from the Trees to See the Forest

Your team members likely seek the same autonomy and authority that you've achieved in moving beyond the concrete wall, which leads me to my next point. Get comfortable relinquishing control of the details and ask for help when you need it. This may be tough if you're used to doing it all.

Earlier in your career, it may have made sense to know every moving part of a project. While it can be hard to let go and stop exercising the technical skills that made you a great candidate in the first place, being a manager requires a new level of support—more listening and guiding others than doing.

When assigning projects to your direct reports, avoid the urge to micromanage. Give them a goal, a deadline, and clear expectations. Then let them figure out how to achieve that goal, reach that deadline, and meet those expectations. This will free up space for you to observe. Pay attention to their strengths, challenge areas, and motivations, and provide them with the support they need to succeed. In doing so, you can delegate meaningful projects to each person while also creating a culture of continuous feedback.

To pull your focus away from the "how," it also helps to think about ways you can make the team work better as a collective. For instance, instead of taking the reins when someone is falling behind, use your energy to troubleshoot and improve workflows. Plan quarterly goals for each person and the team as a whole in advance. Create a predictable communication cadence, including regular check-ins and guardrails for feedback.

Now that you've finally arrived in a new position, this is your chance to make an impact on the bigger picture and allow your team members to grow in their own way.

Cultivate a Community

Companies ramping up their diversity, equity, and inclusion efforts are keen on creating a sense of belonging—an employee's perception of acceptance within a given group. As a new leader, try creating a community instead.

Stanford University has a nice explanation of the difference:

> Although "belonging" includes an individual's sense of connection to and personal identification with the whole, "community" embraces an individual's participation and belief in something larger than themselves. Creating and supporting a thriving community involves both collectively establishing a group's values and norms and respecting the importance and responsibility of every individual in contributing to a shared vision and the daily life of that common good.[3]

Building rapport goes beyond knowing your teammates' professional goals. It's about creating a psychologically safe environment. Schedule weekly one-on-ones with each of your direct reports and use a part of this time to better understand how their personal lives affect how they show up to work. The advice here is not to spend half an hour discussing your social life but, rather, to check in with people on both a professional and a personal level. Make them feel seen, appreciated, and heard as a human being, not just a worker.

For instance, how many children does a person have? How is their work-life balance? What cultural holidays do they need space to honor or celebrate? Do they feel that their work has value? Do they understand how their tasks are contributing to the larger organization? Even questions about what Netflix series they'd recommend or what books they're currently reading can show people that you care about their tastes and interests, and help to build an inclusive space.

In a hybrid work environment where Slack or Microsoft Teams are the new watercoolers, tapping into the human side of the business—and sending a meme or two—clears the way for innovation with working relationships centered on understanding and respect.

. . .

My advice above all: Give yourself grace. Even as the diversity industry continues to grow, underrepresented talent remains stuck in the middle, with fewer growth opportunities or senior executive pathways. In breaking the concrete wall, you've made it through an immense systemic challenge passed down from the generations before us.

QUICK RECAP

What should you do when you step into a managerial position for the first time? Here are three lessons from a first-time, first-generation manager:

- Confidence is a cornerstone of leadership. Whenever you feel unsure of yourself as a new leader, take a moment to remember your unique skills and wins.

- Get comfortable relinquishing control of the details and ask for help when you need it. Listen and guide others, rather than taking the reins yourself.

- Create a community with your team by building rapport and a psychologically safe environment for all. Get to know your reports on a professional and a personal level.

Adapted from "Leading as a First-Time, First-Generation Manager," on hbr.org, October 21, 2021.

Building Relationships and Trust

4

Encouraging Your Team to Be Open with You

by Amanda Reill

When you become a manager, the power dynamics with your former peers will inevitably shift. You're now responsible for evaluating their performance. Their job security is contingent on you. Your relationships will, and should, change.

For example, you may notice a shift in the way your direct reports give you information. While the individuals on your team may have once felt comfortable casually sharing their frustrations with you, that may no longer be the case when you step into a management role. The founder of Pixar, Ed Catmull, addresses this reality in his book *Creativity, Inc.*—the story of Pixar's company culture from its early beginnings to the strength it holds today. He said, "It simply doesn't occur to [new managers] that after they get promoted to a leadership position, no one is going to come out and say, 'Now that you are a manager, I can no longer be candid with you.' Instead, many new leaders assume, wrongly, that their access to information is unchanged."

This is a major challenge for managers. But access to water-cooler information—what employees are disgruntled about, what ideas they wish leadership would listen to, what systems aren't working—is critical to your success.

So, how do you maintain trust? How do you make sure your team still feels comfortable walking up to you and voicing their opinions?

Notice When Things Go Silent

When you're a manager, you may notice that the frustrations your team feels about their work, company leadership—or you—go silent. And those frustrations are valuable data to you as a leader. But to assume no news is good news is not a wise option. Instead, start with the assumption that your watercooler badge has been taken away.

The sentiment, "For sure, boss! All good over here!" comes from people who are interested in keeping their jobs and not making waves. Being honest about frustrations in the workplace can be a risky endeavor, after all. Though we optimistically hope that we've created a safe place for people to challenge the status quo, when 36% of people are worried about losing their jobs, the reality is a bit trickier than that.[1]

Team health depends on honest feedback. If people keep their frustrations quiet, they may begin to lean toward quietly quitting or leaving the team altogether. This is one reason it's imperative for managers to create "psychological safety," a term coined by Harvard Business School professor Amy Edmondson that she sums up as "a belief that one will not be punished or humiliated for speaking up with ideas, questions, concerns, or mistakes, and that the team is safe for interpersonal risk-taking."[2]

How do you establish psychological safety with your team, which may now feel that being honest with you is a bit more risky?

Address the Elephant in the Room

If you're new to your role, try to address the new power differential within the first one or two weeks. Explain to your team what success looks like in your new role, how it depends on the team, and how much you want to continue to collaborate with them, support them, and help them grow.

You might say something like, "Hey folx, I wanted to gather everyone together to talk about this next season for our team. I have a different role now and I want to use it to make things better. I don't want to lose your trust in the process, and I want you to know that I'm committed to creating a psychologically safe work environment where we feel comfortable speaking candidly, disagreeing, and sharing ideas without fear of repercussions."

If you've been in your role for a while and are just now noticing a change in openness, schedule a meeting with your team to establish some ground rules for feedback. It's important to create a smooth runway for people to provide feedback by telling them where and when you plan to collect it. Can they send you their feedback via email, put it in a feedback box, walk up to you during the open-door hour, or share it over Slack?

Some may have their reasons for being uncomfortable sharing their views directly. Maybe they're more comfortable with giving it anonymously or sharing it via another person because of your power differential. Provide alternative routes for communication if they're having trouble communicating with you for any reason. This could be a designated person in HR, another manager, a team lead, or anyone else you trust to act as a responsible mediator.

Take Yellow Flags Seriously

People give you information about their temperature every day. When an employee begins exhibiting red-flag signals that they're not happy, it could be too late. Learn to look for yellow flags. Here are a few:

- Pay attention to facial expressions on Zoom and follow up with people individually when something seems off. You could say, "Hey, I noticed you didn't seem quite yourself this morning—just wanted to check in and see if you were doing OK or if you had additional thoughts about the meeting."

- Assume that anything anyone does tell you is the tip of an iceberg. If someone brings a complaint to you, such as a difficulty with a coworker, there is a chance they're holding back so they don't seem disgruntled. Validating their concerns is important to understanding if the situation is worse than they're letting on. You could ask, "How long have you been feeling that way?" or "What else have you noticed?" to see if the person has more to share.

- Any change in behavior is worth wondering about, such as a change in someone's schedule, a lack of eye contact, or uncharacteristic quietness. Something like quietness isn't a negative signal in and of itself, but the key is noticing whether something has changed. The behavior change may have nothing to do with work, but when you check in, the person may share with you a personal struggle that you'll be glad you're aware of.

The best way to handle yellow flags is with empathy and validation. Raising a concern feels risky, so your team members need to know that they can trust you before they'll be willing to share their concerns. Start by acknowledging the person's courage and initiative in trying to deal with a sticky situation or for opening up to you. Make sure you hear them out entirely before beginning to problem-solve, explain, or defend. For instance, if someone on your team has felt uncomfortable with the way a client was treating them, don't be quick to dismiss it before hearing them out. You can say, "I know it was probably not easy for you to bring this up, but I'm so thankful you did. I can understand why that would be uncomfortable."

When possible, don't neglect the power of an apology. After thoroughly listening, consider whether you can offer an apology to the person for ways the company could have supported them better. For instance, in the case described earlier, trying to create a zero-tolerance policy for toxic clients and showing your employees that they are more important than the bottom line would give you an opportunity to "put your money where your mouth is."

Optimize Your EQ

Emotional intelligence (EQ) is our ability to perceive, interpret, and manage our own emotions, as well as recognize and influence the emotions of those around us. It acknowledges that humans aren't machines, and they bring their emotions with them to work every day. An effective manager has a good understanding of *how* these emotions impact their team's work and leads their team in collective EQ upskilling.

As you work to build trust and openness on your team, meet regularly to hone your collective EQ. Explore the following questions together:

- What personalities, communication styles, and working styles are present on our team?

- What do you each need from me as a manager and from each other as teammates?

- What processes do we currently use for resolving conflict, providing feedback, and generating ideas? How comfortable are we with disagreements?

- How good is our team with managing failure?

Gather the team's answers to these questions, identify areas of improvement, and set some goals.

For instance, you may discover that your team feels like there's a lack of consistency in how new ideas are rolled out in the organization. Maybe they're not sure when and where to provide their opinions about changes that impact their individual workflows. Or perhaps there's a disconnect between your leaders and those who implement their visions, meaning you need to build a stronger communication bridge.

Once you're aware of these issues—whatever they may be—you can take steps to resolve them. This often starts by recognizing each person's strengths and challenge areas, respecting them, and establishing workflows that benefit everyone. Sometimes it may also involve giving feedback to stakeholders outside of your team, particularly if the problem is trickling down from leadership.

. . .

The most important thing to remember when moving to managing people is that the dynamic *will* change. It has to. Addressing that fact up front and establishing new, trusting relationships with your colleagues will give you the best chance at a cohesive, transparent team moving forward.

QUICK RECAP

Access to information about what isn't working is critical to a manager's success. But how can you encourage your team to give you that information?

- Don't assume that no news is good news. You must establish psychological safety, so your team feels safe being honest with you.

- Create a smooth runway for people to provide feedback by telling them where and when you plan to collect it.

- Pay attention to signs that something may be off with your direct reports, such as facial expressions, uncharacteristic quietness, or schedule changes.

- As you work to build trust and openness on your team, meet regularly to hone your collective emotional intelligence.

Adapted from "Encouraging Your Team to Be Open with You (as a New Manager)," on hbr.org, July 4, 2023.

5

Five Ways Leaders (Accidentally) Erode Trust

by Ron Carucci

As a manager, your top priority is establishing trust with your team. Your direct reports must have confidence in your ability to make decisions, communicate effectively, and help them grow in order to perform to the best of their abilities.

But establishing trust takes time, and the natural stressors of being a people leader can make it even harder. If you're not careful, your efforts to prove yourself as a capable leader may end up eroding, rather than strengthening, the foundation of trust you aim to build. And depending on how you arrived in your new role—promoted from within the team, brought in from another department, or hired from outside the company—you may face unique circumstances that make this process even more challenging.

Here are five common ways leaders unwittingly erode trust and how to avoid them.

Using Your Expertise to Coach or Help

One of the hardest things to do as a manager is to let go of the expertise and work that set you apart as an individual contributor. This is especially precarious when you are promoted from within your team or organization.

When leading people who do the work that you once did, it's easy to want to hold them to the standard you performed at. Your ability to do this work well is likely how you distinguished yourself and got your promotion. You may fear that if your direct reports aren't able to do the work as well as you did, it will reflect poorly on your leadership. In addition, the intangible aspects of leadership may make you unconsciously miss the tasks that you once found deeply gratifying—and that your team members are now responsible for.

As a result, you may be tempted to handhold, over-coach, or even do the work for them to demonstrate what you're looking for. But others rarely experience this as helpful. It can instead make them feel inadequate or see you as a micromanager. Once your team believes that you don't trust them with their work, they'll struggle to trust you with their growth and learning.

What to do instead

Help your direct reports master their tasks and projects in their own way. Assess their abilities against yours when you *started* doing the work—when you were first learning. Use your expertise judiciously, avoiding comparisons or being overly corrective.

You can say something like, "Tell me how I can best use my experience in this work to help you grow."

Be clear about your expectations around deliverables, key performance indicators, and deadlines. Agree on the outcomes you both believe they can achieve, and the approach they feel most comfortable taking (versus mimicking yours). Then, let them figure out how to achieve the goals you set, leveraging your guidance when they need it.

Trying to Build Rapport and a Sense of Egalitarianism

Many leaders struggle with the resulting power differential that occurs when they become a manager. This can be even more challenging if you're promoted from within your team and your former peers are now your direct reports. It can create a feeling of awkwardness and distance with individuals you previously felt close to.

To combat the discomfort, many leaders go out of their way to retain the same sense of rapport they once enjoyed as peers. This creates challenges later when you suddenly have to exercise your authority. Trying to pretend that things haven't changed that much won't help you build trust.

The hard truth is that once you become a leader, the relational boundaries with your former peers must shift. Similarly, if you were hired from the outside, you must set appropriate boundaries with your new team members. Your ability to socialize with them, what information you share with them, and what information they share with you must be carefully thought through.

What you can do instead

If you were promoted from within your company, having a proactive conversation with each person with whom your relationship has changed will enable you to clarify what they can expect from you as their leader. It also curtails the natural temptation they may have to curry favor with you or to leverage your past relationship for their personal gain. You might say something like, "I don't want the fact that we now share a reporting relationship to be awkward for us. But the reality is that some things must shift between us for us both to be successful. Let's talk about what parts of our relationship can stay intact and what parts we'll need to adapt."

If you were hired from the outside or are managing entirely new team members, start with a conversation that sets mutual expectations. You might begin with something like, "In new relationships, I find it helpful to share my expectations of others and to clarify their expectations of me as their leader. That way, we can do our best to help each other be successful."

Trying to Build Confidence by Looking Confident

Plenty of research shows that people are drawn to confidence in a leader. Many new leaders try to mask their insecurities by donning a leadership persona to appear confident. They speak in more declarative sentences, are overtly positive, and offer reassurances in the face of uncertainties.

But overconfidence can sometimes have the opposite effect, diluting trust by coming across as overly self-reliant, inauthentic, and out of touch. Yes, those you lead need to know you have confidence in yourself. But they also need to trust that you have confidence in *them* by acknowledging the areas where you aren't as strong and will need their help.

What you can do instead

Your confidence, in appropriate measure, is only one characteristic of leadership that will strengthen trust. If you rely on it excessively, you risk losing that trust when tough conditions make confidence impossible. You must balance confidence with humility, authenticity, and vulnerability so that the trust you earn is well-rounded and grounded in your full humanity. In the face of uncertainties—sudden strategic pivots, budget shortfalls, project setbacks—your team needs to know you are comfortable not having all the answers.

For example, one newly appointed leader I coached inherited a project that was way behind and had ballooned in scope. The team was frustrated, as was her boss. Feeling the pressure to get things on track quickly and reestablish the team's confidence, she was tempted to step in and start directing people on what to do. I urged her to instead consider that the team might find it more confidence-building if she acknowledged how tough things had been and engaged the team in coming up with solutions. This helped reestablish their self-confidence while also making them trust that she could listen and learn.

Checking In to Make Sure Everyone Is OK

If you tend to be a people-pleaser, you will be especially prone to this misstep. As you build relationships with your direct reports, checking in with them to see how they are adapting to your leadership and if you have to make any adjustments is a good idea. It's a great way to calibrate and demonstrate you are willing to modify if needed. It will build trust in your commitment to putting their needs first.

But in excess, these check-ins can begin to erode trust among your team members, particularly if you get defensive or don't act on their feedback. They may start to see your inquiries as manipulative and self-serving. When this happens, they may try to accommodate you by saying things are fine, further eroding their trust in your ability to make improvements.

What to do instead

Before seeking feedback from your team members, ask yourself if you're motivated by an actual desire to learn and adjust, or an unconscious need for validation and reassurance. While it's a good idea to invite feedback, you also want to empower your direct reports to initiate feedback conversations with you when they are feeling frustrated. This builds trust in your openness to their feedback by both soliciting it and inviting them to initiate it.

If you sense that someone you lead is feeling frustrated or unsatisfied, be specific in your inquiry and keep it focused on them. You might say something like, "I sense that something is frustrating you. Is there any way I can be helpful?" If they respond with a curt "No, I'm fine," then leave it with a simple "OK, I understand. But please know that, if something changes, I hope you'll let me know."

Too many new leaders, anxious to keep things harmonious, jump right to questions like, "Have I done something to upset you?" with the assumption that whatever's bothering the person is about them. This risks eroding trust by conveying that you are overly self-involved rather than genuinely concerned about them.

Building Credibility Through Past Successes

As a leader, you need to build credibility. You may be tempted to rely on your track record of positive results to make people trust your decision-making and leadership abilities. But overly relying on your past usually backfires. Leaders who have been hired from outside their current organization should be hyper-aware of this mishap.

Resist starting sentences with, "Well, when I was at XYZ company, we approached this . . ." People will accept one or two mentions of your past experiences because they know you don't have any other frame of reference. But after a while, they may start to hear it as an indictment of their approach and ideas. It can erode trust in your ability to adapt and work with others in this new context to find suitable solutions.

What to do instead

Whether you were promoted from within the organization or hired from outside, avoid leaning too much on your past successes. A better source of credibility and, therefore, trust is your curiosity. Ask your team questions about how they've tried to address current challenges or what ideas they've felt haven't been heard before. This gives you a body of knowledge that you can *build on* with your experience and enables you to contextualize past successes in the current situation. By demonstrating your willingness to adapt your ideas while learning from your team, you're more likely to build trust.

.   .   .

Building and maintaining trust with your team is a long process. While you may be anxious about performing well in your role, it's important not to rush things. Listen to your feelings of anxiety and self-doubt, but don't let them weaken trust on your team. Stay focused on your larger goal of genuinely earning trust over time with your full humanity, experience, and desire to make your direct reports as successful as they can be.

QUICK RECAP

Here are five common ways managers unwittingly erode trust on their teams:

- **Using your expertise to coach or help.** Avoid micromanaging your direct reports; instead, help them master their projects in their own way.

- **Trying to build rapport and a sense of egalitarianism.** Talk with each person on your team to clarify what they can expect from you.

- **Trying to build confidence by looking confident.** Balance confidence with humility, authenticity, and vulnerability.

- **Checking in to make sure everyone is OK.** Before seeking feedback, ask yourself if you actually want to learn and adjust, or simply need reassurance.

- **Building credibility through past successes.** Lead with curiosity, rather than over-relying on your past achievements.

Adapted from "5 Ways New Leaders (Accidentally) Erode Trust on Their Teams," on hbr.org, March 18, 2024.

How do you repair trust on your team if you've lost it?
Watch this video to find out:

6

When You Can't Be Transparent with Your Team

by Ramona Shaw

There are many books and classes that describe leadership as a set of skills anyone can pick up over time. Things like listening and communication, time management, and conducting effective one-on-ones are just a handful of competencies that great leaders have. However, there is one significant skill that is often less talked about and even more difficult to learn: managing your emotions as someone in a position of power who has access to more information than others.

This is a dilemma many managers face: You know something that could impact your team, but you can't share it. How do you balance your values with your words and actions as a leader?

A client of mine recently faced this. She learned that she had to lay off 30% of her direct reports and that her boss would be replaced one week before she had to share the news with her team. When we spoke, she told me how emotional it was. She was upset about talented people being let go, worried about the morale and workload of the employees left behind, stressed about having a new boss, and in general, anxious about communicating a decision that was out of her control.

All of her emotions were valid. None of what she expressed was an indication of weakness or incompetence. Still, she wondered: Would senior leadership notice that she was having trouble staying focused? If she shared hints about what was coming, would it create uncertainty for her team and compromise her job? Should she question senior leadership, and if she did, would they think she didn't understand the big picture? Would her team lose trust and respect for her? Would people adapt with an open mindset?

This is a challenge that, as a manager, you will face time and again—whether it's a layoff, a reorganization, or a shift in your company's business initiatives. The good news is that there are ways to gracefully navigate it, and you should learn them. A growing body of research shows that when leaders leave their emotions unchecked, they make lower-quality decisions and negatively impact team performance, work culture, and employee motivation.[1]

Here are a few tips to help you stay true to your leadership responsibilities despite the emotional challenge of hearing news you can't (yet) share with your team.

Remember That Your Job as a Leader Is to Represent the Company

Something many new managers overlook is that, as a leader of your organization, your job is to represent the organization. This comes with both spoken and unspoken responsibilities.

When you're privy to new information that you're not allowed to share with your team, you may feel pulled in two directions. As a manager, you're expected to represent the leadership team, but as an empathetic human being, you may also be tempted to prioritize your personal needs and relationships over the interests of the business. Your job is to choose the former—to consider what the organization and your team need from you as a leader right now. If you choose to focus instead on what's best for your relationships, you risk leaking confidential information and eroding trust with the leadership team or potentially even losing your job.

Most often this dilemma occurs when there's a conflict between the information you learn and your personal values. If you're facing that conflict, try this exercise: Picture yourself in two different roles—the role of a leader and the role of a friend. Communicate with your team as a leader and extend compassion and patience as a friend.

For example, if you're being asked about rumors surrounding a layoff that you're unable to disclose, you could say, "There's nothing further I can communicate at this point, unfortunately. But I understand that these rumors are concerning. I feel the same way. Whatever happens, I will do my best to support you and the team. In the meantime, how can I be of help?"

Ground Yourself in Your Values and Principles

Good leaders are prepared leaders, and this includes having the ability to anticipate challenges. A clear set of values and principles will help you make good decisions, especially when you're feeling pulled in different directions. Don't wait for a difficult situation to land in your lap to figure out what principles guide you.

Take a moment now to consider what values you would want to honor should you find yourself in a situation where you have more information than you're allowed to share. Ask yourself:

- What do you stand for as a leader?

- How would you like others to describe your leadership style?

- What do you expect from your coworkers?

- Which of your personality traits are you most proud of?

- Which leaders do you admire most and why?

If transparency is a value of yours, a leadership principle connected to that might be to honor transparent communication both upward and downward (with your boss and with your employees). If you're unable to honor that, how will you address the friction you feel?

In this situation, I would advise people to consider all of their values. Perhaps, for instance, your other values are family, trustworthiness, and loyalty. How would making a compromise impact those aspects of your character? Would you lose your job and be unable to support your loved ones? Would you give up your reputation as a trustworthy team member and leader? Or could you make a compromise that would help you stay true to your values while also honoring your commitments to your employer?

For instance, you could tell a worried team member that you're unable to share information at this time but promise to do so as soon as you can and offer to talk through their anxious feelings. Often, there is a way to meet yourself—and others—in the middle.

If you're in a situation where you have information that violates your values, or may be unethical or discriminatory in any way, it's also your responsibility as a leader to do what you believe is right. You should discuss the situation with your manager or with your HR representative.

Share Your Principles with Others

Having a clear leadership philosophy that both you and your team understand—including a set of core values and principles—will not only help you make the best decision (for you), but it will also help you communicate it clearly to others.

For example, if 30% of my client's team members are laid off and a remaining employee were to ask my client if she knew about it beforehand, my client could concisely and clearly communicate the reason for her decision, letting her value of transparency guide her:

> Yes, I received a heads-up from senior leadership. While transparency is really important to me, I had to take all aspects into consideration when deciding what information to share with you and other team members. To share the confidential information I was given sooner than I was permitted would have had serious consequences for both the business and me. I really wish I could have been fully transparent with you and everyone else, and my

goal is still to support you in any way I can. I hope you can understand what I based my decision on, knowing that there was no easy way to go about it. I understand it's not easy to hear this, and I'm here if you want to talk more about it or if you have more questions.

By stating your values and principles, your employees will likely feel a greater sense of trust and confidence in you because they'll recognize the thoughtful and proactive approach you took in making the decision.

Prioritize Respect Over Being Liked

You are in good company if you desire to be both liked and respected at work. The majority of us strive to feel appreciated and recognized on a team. These are basic human needs. But there will be times when you, as a leader, have to make tough decisions that not everyone will support. It's normal for some people to dislike you temporarily as a result.

If you lose sight of this and make decisions to be liked or to avoid hard calls, you will likely lose respect. Trying to lead a team that doesn't respect you or doesn't have confidence that you'll do what's right or what's best for their careers, even if it gets tough, will be a very difficult endeavor.

Bear this in mind when you feel tempted to say something or do something only to be liked or to prevent interpersonal tension. When you're able to manage your emotions, you're able to do the hard and right thing, instead of the easy and wrong thing. That will garner you respect.

Think Longer Term

In high-stress moments, it's easy to overlook the long-term perspective. Many of us tend to prioritize our short-term needs over our long-term gains. But trusted and respected leaders know that sharing confidential information to alleviate tension that they, alone, are experiencing, is ultimately more harmful than productive. It erodes trust and respect from senior leadership, peers, and employees alike. Particularly if you don't have all the details, sharing information with your team too soon can cause a whirlpool of stress and confusion. Typically, it's not worth it.

Let's take my client's situation as an example. If she had told someone on her team that layoffs were coming, but that she wasn't supposed to say anything, the recipient of that news may have initially felt appreciative and trusted her, but after that first rush of relief, secondary thoughts would have likely come up. The recipient may have wondered if they could ever trust their manager with confidential information of their own. They may also have worried about what else was said or done behind their back, or spread the confidential information to other people, following their manager's example.

Losing integrity at the expense of sharing confidential information is a common consequence. In the heat of the moment, it's easy to lose sight of that.

Don't Make Promises That You Can't Keep

Last, keep in mind that withholding confidential information for the organization's benefit doesn't mean that you need to invent an alternative story or make promises and commitments that you won't be able to fulfill.

As an example, in the early days of the Covid-19 pandemic, several of my clients shared that their senior leadership teams promised them that no layoffs would happen. But as the weeks went by, and the severity of the situation became clearer, my clients were faced with both furloughs and layoffs. These changes made sense for the businesses, but employee-manager trust was eroded in the process.

A better approach in these tricky situations is to be as honest and transparent as you can without leaking information. You could say, "While this may change, as of today, we've communicated that no layoffs are taking place," or, "I can't promise you a future decision, but what I can promise you is that I've got your back and will support you through any change that may come our way."

· · ·

Applying these six tips won't make your situation feel less emotional. In fact, demonstrating emotional maturity and being comfortable with the uncomfortable may be harder in the short term. But once the intensity dies down, the news is out, and this phase is over, you will have stayed true to your values and earned trust and respect that will benefit you for years to come.

QUICK RECAP

If you know something that could impact your team but you can't share it, how do you balance your values with your actions as a leader?

- Remember that your job as a leader is to represent the company.

- Determine how you will address the friction you feel by leaning into your values.

- Share your values with your employees to increase their trust and confidence in you.

- Accept that there will be times when you must make decisions that everyone may not support.

- Think longer term—sharing information too soon can cause a whirlpool of stress and confusion.

- Don't make promises or commitments that you can't keep.

Adapted from content posted on hbr.org, March 14, 2023.

For more on trust and transparency, listen to this podcast:

Setting Team Norms

7

Dear Manager, You're Holding Too Many Meetings

by Benjamin Laker, Vijay Pereira, Ashish Malik, and Lebene Soga

Meetings serve different purposes, ranging from informal social gatherings to formal strategy discussions. They often show up on our calendars as recurring events (with no end date in sight). New research shows that about 70% of all meetings keep employees from working and completing all their tasks. While there was a 20% decrease in the average length of meetings during the Covid-19 pandemic, the number of meetings attended by a worker on average rose by 13.5%.[1] Ineffective meetings that waste our time can negatively impact psychological, physical, and mental well-being.[2]

Our recent research found that newly promoted managers may be contributing to the problem. New managers hold almost a third (29%) more meetings than their seasoned counterparts.[3] When we set out to understand the hidden costs of flexible working practices, we discovered that meetings have steadily increased in frequency and duration since companies transitioned to the remote workplace.

There are a couple of reasons this might be the case. Without the ability to connect with their team members in person as often, people newly promoted into management roles may feel extra pressure to build connections digitally. And they may be driven by a desire to be more visible and get buy-in from their teams. It's also easier than ever to stack our days with back-to-back meetings. When we're working remotely, we don't have to travel between private meeting rooms. We can pretty much leave one meeting and log into another a minute later.

What's the impact? Our research shows that 92% of employees consider meetings costly and unproductive.[4] And countless online interactions can lead to "Zoom fatigue"—a condition neuropsychologists say is a big contributor to "technostress."[5] In short, more meetings don't help *anyone* reach their goals.

To investigate further, and consider the implications for managers, we surveyed 76 companies that reduced the number of meetings over the course of 14 months. We found that although building trust and achieving cohesion rely on the frequency and quality of a team's interactions, meetings are no longer the best way for managers to accomplish those things. In fact, there are much more effective ways to develop bonds in the absence of face-to-face meetings—including having *fewer* meetings altogether.

The Benefits of Having Fewer Meetings

Across the 76 companies we surveyed, we found that employee productivity was 71% higher when meetings were reduced by 40%. This is largely because employees felt more empowered and autonomous. Rather than a schedule being the boss, they owned their to-do lists and held themselves accountable, which consequently increased their satisfaction by 52%. (See figure 7-1.)

Removing 60% of meetings increased cooperation by 55%. Workers found better ways to connect one-on-one at a pace suitable for them, often using project management tools, such as Slack or Teams, to aid communications specific to each project. In doing so, the risk of stress decreased by 57%, which improved employees' overall well-being.

When meetings declined by 80%, we found that employees' perception that they were being micromanaged lessened by 74%. People felt valued, trusted, and more engaged, subsequently working harder for their company. Communication was 65% clearer and substantially more effective. The reason is that there were far fewer misunderstandings. To review an assignment or request, people would quickly check a previous Slack conversation or a project outline. The often-used phrases "I thought you told me . . ." or "I was under the impression . . ." were rarely used.

How to Scale Back Meetings

If you're a manager trying to establish healthy and impactful team norms, we have some advice to help you rethink your

FIGURE 7-1

Impact of fewer meetings

A survey of 76 companies that reduced their meetings over the course of 14 months found that overall employee ratings were positively impacted.

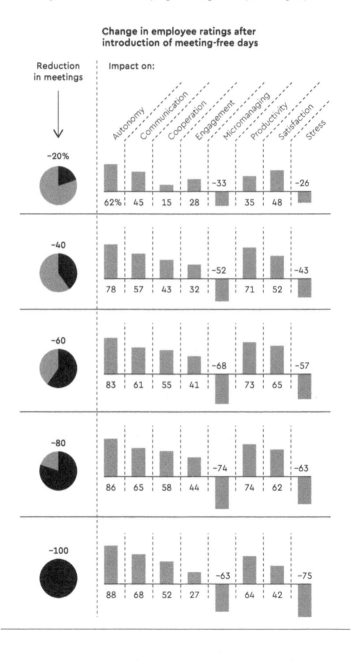

Change in employee ratings after introduction of meeting-free days

approach. By following our suggestions, nearly half of the companies we investigated reduced meetings by 40% over a three-month period. Thirty-five percent achieved three no-meeting days per week, and 11% achieved four.

Be *very* selective

Think about the meetings you've conducted or participated in recently. Which ones have been the most useful? You're probably thinking about a new project launch or a brainstorm that required a two-way dialogue in real time. As a general rule of thumb, we recommend holding meetings only when absolutely necessary. That typically includes:

- To review work that's occurred (what worked or didn't and why)

- To clarify and validate something (policies, team goals, and so on)

- To distribute work appropriately among your team

Even in those cases, you should carefully edit your invite list. Is *everyone* really needed? Or can you make the meeting optional for some people? The less important the topic is to their work, the less engaged your team members will be.

Encourage your team to flag or cancel meetings if they aren't the best use of their time. Make it clear that, as their manager, you encourage it and won't judge or punish them. Being judicious about which meetings add value and which don't will help free up people's calendars. Doing so also forces managers to rethink the informal ad hoc engagements that pepper everybody's calendars.

Interestingly, we found this strategy garners loyalty toward managers. Granting autonomy allows people to job craft, which previous studies show helps them find meaning in their work.[6]

Transition your daily status meetings to Slack or Teams

Daily huddles are the most frequently held meetings, and often, they are the most difficult to give up. As a new manager, you may feel that it's important for your team members to be aware of one another's work in order to reach your goals as a group. These meetings may seem like the best time to do this.

We have another suggestion: Set up a Slack or Teams channel specifically for this purpose. Every weekday, schedule a message to go out at 9:00 a.m.: "@here What's on your plate today?"

Ask your team members to respond within the hour, explaining what they're working on, any important project updates, setbacks, and so on. Managers (and your team members) can then scan the responses and follow up privately on updates that may need more context.

Our research found that 83% of employees preferred using these chat touch points over traditional one-to-one meetings because it saved them time. If your team members have a question, they can drop you a message instead of having to find a 30-minute block on your calendar.

Make the Most of Your One-on-One Meetings

by Steven G. Rogelberg

The best managers recognize that one-on-ones, or regular meetings with your direct reports, are not an add-on to their role—they are foundational to it. Those who fully embrace these meetings as the place where leadership happens can make their teams' day-to-day output better and more efficient, build trust and psychological safety, and improve employees' experiences, motivation, and engagement.

But how can you prepare for and facilitate effective one-on-ones?

Create an Agenda Before the Meeting

Both direct reports and managers should contribute to the agenda of a one-on-one so that both your priorities, and your employee's concerns, can be addressed. Collaborating on an agenda can be as simple as having each party create a list of topics to discuss.

Alternatively, some managers create the agenda from broad questions, such as: What would you like to talk about today? How are things going with you and your team? What are your current priorities, and are there any problems or concerns you would like to talk through? Is there anything I can help you with or anywhere I can better support you? What do I need to know about or understand from your perspective?

But don't focus too much on immediate tactical issues and fires to be put out. Periodically weave in longer-horizon topics such as career planning and developmental opportunities—by either taking five or 10 minutes at every meeting to discuss those areas or dedicating one out of every three or four meetings to addressing them.

Listen More Than You Talk

Once you've prepared for a meeting, a fruitful discussion will depend on your ability to create a setting in which your employee feels comfortable. A valuable one-on-one addresses both the practical needs and the personal needs—to feel respected, heard, valued, trusted, and included—of the employee.

Make sure to actively listen as your direct report speaks. Display genuine interest without judgment and acknowledge the employee's viewpoint even if you disagree with it. Ask questions that clarify and constructively challenge that viewpoint. Encourage your team member to provide thoughts on the matters at hand and potential solutions to problems. Stay vigilant about your body language and reactions to ensure that you're creating a welcoming and safe space.

Improve Your Meetings Over Time

Ideally, both parties should leave the conversation feeling valued, respected, and well-informed, with clarity about next steps on projects, solutions to problems, and the commitments that each of them has made. However, the most important metric for success is whether your employee found the meeting both valuable tactically and fulfilling personally.

To learn where you stand and to improve these meetings over time, start by asking your team members for feedback and ideas to make future one-on-ones better. Or you can anonymously survey your team with three basic questions: What's going well with the one-on-ones? What's not going well? Do you have ideas for improving them?

———

Excerpted from "Make the Most of Your One-on-One Meetings," *Harvard Business Review*, November–December 2022 (product #R2206L).

Use digital tools for asynchronous work

The next time you have a brainstorming meeting, ask, *Can some of this be done asynchronously?* The answer is probably yes.

For example, tools like Mural and Google Forms can be used to get people to submit their ideas in advance. Then you can schedule a follow-up meeting to review them together, likely cutting your meeting time in half. Eighty-three percent of employees in our survey preferred this approach over traditional methods, claiming it helps them contribute on their own time and further refine ideas in person.

Additionally, meeting-dependent activities like checking in on the progress of projects can be tracked asynchronously on a dashboard in a way that is transparent to everyone. This approach, we found, can help prune calendars, leaving more space for valuable "no meeting" time and focused work.

. . .

Whereas our data highlights the importance of holding fewer meetings, we want to emphasize that managers need to understand what works for their unique contexts to maximize the full benefits of these strategies. For example, we found that the advantages of no-meeting periods begin to plateau after reducing meetings by 60% and actually wane beyond that. Satisfaction, productivity, engagement, and cooperation all decline when meetings are reduced completely, instead of retaining at least one day for meetings. We posit that when two days per week are retained for meetings, it can prove beneficial.

Even so, with the traditional meetings yielding little return on time investment, the opportunity cost is too high not to act now. Your teams are full of talented and capable people doing what they do best, but they need space to do so. By better understanding how they want to work together, how meetings fit into that, and where meetings do and don't add value, you'll minimize the need for useless meetings.

QUICK RECAP

If you're a manager trying to establish healthy and impactful team norms, start by rethinking your approach to meetings.

- **Be selective when scheduling meetings.** Don't schedule one unless you need to review work that's occurred, clarify something significant, or distribute work.

- **Transition your daily status meetings to Slack or Teams.** Use chat touch points instead of traditional one-to-one meetings to save time.

- **Use digital tools for asynchronous work.** Allow team members to contribute to discussions on their own time by using online tools like Mural and Google Forms. Then, further refine ideas in person.

Adapted from content posted on hbr.org, March 9, 2022.

Wondering how to make hybrid meetings work for you and your team? Watch this video:

Don't Let Poor Communication Slow Down Your Team

by Gleb Tsipursky

As more and more employees are working remotely or in hybrid work environments, the need for effective communication has become even stronger.

In a recent report by FlexOS, employees rated their managers a mediocre seven out of 10—the equivalent of a C, if graded—on effectively managing hybrid and remote teams. Worse, 30% said they're frustrated by unclear communication from their bosses.[1] Some of these challenges certainly come from the more siloed communication environment created by remote and hybrid work.

As a manager, it's your job to establish communication norms for your team. When managers are unclear in their communication, it can rob teams of their focus, diluting the overall quality of their output. Managers need to realize that clear, consistent communication isn't optional; it's imperative. Poor communication impedes both individual and collective progress.

So how can you become an excellent communicator in this ever-changing work environment?

Set Expectations Up Front

One of the challenges that can come with communicating remotely is information overload. We're all constantly getting bombarded with emails, Slack messages, phone calls, and the like. Align with your team on the optimal use of these various communication platforms. For example, while email may be suited for formal correspondence and long-term directives, instant messaging apps like Microsoft Teams or Slack can handle immediate needs and quick clarifications.

Being aligned as a team on which tool to use and when can significantly reduce communication friction. Consistently stick to the standards you set and remind others if they slip up.

Consider Creating a "Clarity Canvas"

When starting a new project together as a team, create a set of documents that succinctly outlines project goals, individual responsibilities, process instructions, and key deadlines. This centralized hub, which I call a "clarity canvas," affords seamless access to the same reservoir of information and can serve as a touchstone for everyone, averting confusion and minimizing back-and-forths.

Create these documents together—convene all team members, either in person or virtually, and work through each one to ensure you're all on the same page. Through this alignment, not only are comprehension gaps addressed in real time during the canvas-creation phase, but you also lay a robust foundation for process adherence and knowledge dissemination.

Make Everything Accessible

Making sure every team member—remote or in-office—can easily access all communications is nonnegotiable. Keep meticulous records of decisions made, meeting minutes, and project statuses in a centralized digital location accessible to all.

Set standards for where documents are stored and how information is saved. If your organization has access to multiple cloud storage platforms, set rules for what gets uploaded and where. It can also be helpful to provide guidelines for sharing settings to make sure everyone who may need to access the information can find it easily.

Establish Office Hours

One way to facilitate direct communication with your employees is by setting aside official office hours every week—both remotely and in person. This is time when you should be readily accessible via chat, phone, or video call to discuss any concerns or questions. Consider it a virtual open door, so that both in-office and remote employees have equal opportunity for one-on-ones.

There's no need for a specific agenda during this period; just focus on listening empathetically to your staff and addressing their needs. Be fully present. This will make it easier to foster connections with your direct reports.

Do Regular Debriefs

After important company announcements, it can be valuable to set up debrief meetings with your team. Doing so will help you evaluate how well your people understand and accept the announcements and will give you the opportunity to clarify and address any questions. Remember, your team is looking to you to assess how to respond to top-level announcements. You are the mediator of the C-suite's messages to your team.

Bring Everyone Together

A team that plays together stays together. Organizing monthly team-building activities can forge stronger bonds and create a more cohesive team culture. While in-person activities often yield higher emotional engagement, virtual events can also be effective, especially for entirely remote teams.[2] Incorporating these organized interactions serves as a catalyst for open communication by breaking down hierarchical or interpersonal barriers and nurturing an environment where ideas can flow freely among team members. This fosters a culture of transparency and trust, which are foundational for effective communication within a team.

Check In Periodically

It's not wise to assume that no news is good news. One way to check in with your team is to conduct anonymous surveys every month to gauge what activities are resonating with them. Here are some sample questions tailored to gauge the resonance of activities, measure the effectiveness of implemented plans, and nurture an open communication culture:

- Which aspects of the recent communication and collaboration activities did you find most beneficial? Please explain.

- Is there any communication or collaboration activity that you feel didn't resonate well with you? What suggestions do you have for improvements?

- What steps can we take to improve the openness and effectiveness of communication and collaboration within our team?

- Have the recent changes in [specific process or activity] helped in improving your work experience? Please provide examples.

- On a scale of one to 10, how would you rate the effectiveness of the team's communication and collaboration?

Follow this up with a team discussion to interpret the survey results, aiming to balance varied preferences. Once the plan is in motion, don't forget to measure its effectiveness and encourage feedback. Fine-tune the approach each quarter, keeping it ever-responsive to the team's evolving needs. The ensuing discussions from these check-ins and feedback loops can not only give team members a platform to articulate their preferences and concerns, but also foster a culture of open communication. This procedural transparency in addressing and iterating on the team's needs and preferences demonstrates a proactive communication culture, indispensable for nurturing a resilient and adaptive team.

. . .

Communication is not just a soft skill; it's the linchpin of effective management. As you go through this process, don't shy away from leveraging new technologies that can bring your team closer together, both emotionally and operationally. As a new manager, you have the opportunity to reset old ways and establish a more effective role as a communicator in this hybrid and remote landscape.

QUICK RECAP

Clear communication isn't optional; it's imperative. Here are a few tips on improving communication norms with your team:

- Align with your team on the optimal use of the various communication platforms (email, messaging, video calling).

- When starting a new project, create a set of documents that outlines project goals, responsibilities, instructions, and key deadlines.

- Set standards for where documents are stored and how information is saved.

- Establish virtual and in-person office hours for one-on-one discussions.

- After important company announcements, debrief with your team to address any questions.

- Bring everyone together for team-building activities on a regular basis.

- Conduct anonymous surveys every month to measure the effectiveness of your approach.

Adapted from "Poor Communication May Be Slowing Down Your Team," on hbr.org, October 18, 2023.

What to Do When Your Team's Vibe Is Off

by Liane Davey

Is your team feeling stuck, stymied, or just a bit stale? Have you fallen into routines that are no longer serving you? It's OK; teams need occasional course corrections, even in calm waters. And in today's stormy seas, you might need to chart a whole new course as you navigate hybrid work arrangements. The good news is that resetting your team can be easier than you think.

Your first step is to reflect on what feels off. You can think about it in two broad categories. First, is the problem that your team has lost sight of your purpose and the goals you're working toward? If so, your reset will need to focus on realignment. The other possibility (and it could be both) is that you don't feel like a team anymore. Maybe team members feel disconnected, invalidated, or frustrated—so much so that even minor issues are causing conflict. In that case, your reset must focus on revitalizing your team dynamic.

Here's how to navigate both of these approaches.

Realignment

No matter your issue, it's good to begin with realignment. You'll want to prioritize realignment over revitalization for two reasons. First, many team dysfunctions manifest as trust issues when, in fact, they stem from discrepancies in goals, priorities, or expectations. Clearing up those misunderstandings often resolves what you thought were interpersonal issues.

Another reason to start with realignment is that it allows you to tie your reset to external shifts rather than individual behavior problems, making it less likely to trigger defensiveness. When you realign, you're not judging anyone; instead, you're asking how you need to evolve to capitalize on opportunities and mitigate emerging risks. Here are some anchor points for realignment. Choose the ones that best match your situation.

Reset your team's mandate

The first possibility is that your team's purpose needs to evolve. You can explore that possibility with these questions.

- *What external trends require you to adapt?* What are the most salient changes in the external environment, and how do they change the context for your team? For example, if you're a content marketing team, how does ChatGPT change your team's value?

- *How does a shift in company strategy affect your role?* Does your organization have a new vision, strategy, or KPI that

alters what your team needs to deliver? For example, if you're an HR team, does opening European offices require new capabilities or activities?

- *How is your value within the organization evolving?* As organizations grow and change, the role of teams can evolve. How will changes in your organization structure require you to refocus? For example, how will you tailor your offerings if you're an R&D team now supporting two units instead of one?

Reset your team's goals

If your mandate has changed, you'll certainly need to revisit your goals, but even if your purpose is unchanged, your goals might need a refresh. So, consider these as reasons to move the target.

- *How will you build on prior results?* What did you accomplish in the last quarter, and how does that change the trajectory you want for the next few quarters? If you've been achieving your goals, are they ambitious enough? On the other hand, if you've been missing consistently, do you need to lower your goals or risk demoralizing everyone?

- *How will external factors affect your goals?* Is there anything external that might suggest a goal change? For example, do you need to temper expectations in light of an economic downturn, supply chain backlogs, or labor shortages? On the other hand, if your team benefits from

new technological advances, could you accomplish more
than planned?

* *When can you do to Improve your momentum?* Are your goals
  fuzzy, or are your metrics nebulous? Your fastest way to
  improve alignment might be to tighten your definitions
  or tweak your metrics, making it more evident whether
  you're getting traction.

Reset your strategies and tactics

Any changes based on your mandate or goals will necessitate
reexamining your strategies. But don't limit a strategy refresh to
situations where the targets have moved; considering new pos-
sibilities can be a good reset anytime.

* *Are your strategies aligned with your mandate?* If your
  mandate or goals have shifted, how must your strategy
  change in response? For example, if your team has been
  tasked with adding professional services to your software
  offering, what will it take to make that business model
  successful?

* *Where do you need revised tactics?* If you're still working
  toward existing goals, what's been working, and where
  could you change your tack? Conversely, what do you
  need to abandon? Where could you double down?

* *What contingencies might emerge?* Even if you're sticking
  with your existing mandate, goals, strategies, and tactics,

you can reset by considering new scenarios and preparing your contingency plans. What assumptions are embedded in your current plan? What would negate those assumptions? What would be the leading indicators that something is changing?

Reset your roles

It's possible that your team is on the right track, but you're not optimizing the energy and talents of team members. In that case, consider these questions about individuals' accountabilities.

- *Do people need a change in role?* Are there any changes in roles or responsibilities that would make the people on your team more effective? Do you need to change someone's portfolio? Could you shake up who's in what role for multiskilling, development, or succession advantages? Who might be reinvigorated by a new challenge?

- *How could you make accountabilities more straightforward?* Are there opportunities to fine-tune people's responsibilities to make them more compelling? Are there spots where shared accountabilities are diluting people's sense of obligation? How could you increase alignment, efficiency, and effectiveness by clarifying who owns which decisions?

One of the most constructive ways to reset your team is to refocus on what your organization, colleagues, and customers are counting on you to do. Rekindling your team's passion and reminding them what you're fighting for is the best place to start.

Revitalization

The second type of reset is to revitalize your team dynamic. Does it feel like you've devolved from being a true team into a loose collection of people where the whole is no more than the sum of the parts? Or worse, is mistrust or unhealthy conflict making it feel like teamwork is a net negative? In that case, your reset might need to focus less on *what* your team needs to do and more on *how* you do it.

Reset your communication habits

Over time, teams can become lazy and fall into communication patterns that dilute connection. Revisiting your communication habits can help you reconnect.

- *Can you reset your communication channels?* Do you default to certain modes of communication that aren't optimized for the content? For example, if you're using Zoom to inform and email to debate, you've got it backward. Can you use richer communication vehicles for more novel content, contentious discussions, and unfamiliar participants? Can you shunt informational items to email?

- *How could you implement blackout periods?* In addition to the deluge of meetings, most people are also inundated

by a torrent of emails. How could your team enforce
blackout periods when people can turn off notifications
and work without communication obligations? How can
you increase the opportunities for people to work without
distractions?

Reset your team dynamics

There may be times when interpersonal issues and conflict may
be hiding under the surface. In this case, you need to take a closer
look at team dynamics.

- *What would be your new ground rules?* Maybe
  you've had ground rules and stopped respecting
  them, or you never had any. What behaviors have you
  been tolerating that need to stop? What would be
  a welcome addition? Revisiting the principles for
  how team members behave can be an excellent way
  to reset.

- *How could you resolve conflict debts?* If your team has
  been avoiding difficult conversations about priorities and
  trade-offs or trust and disrespect, you need to get the
  issues out in the open to move beyond them.

- *What activities would foster insight into each other?* If your
  team dynamics are suffering, you might want to enlist
  outside help with formal team development activities. For
  example, psychometric tools or group coaching could
  foster trust and promote candor.

If your team is accomplishing plenty but finding it's harder than necessary, these different approaches will jump-start a new, healthier, happier team dynamic.

. . .

As you ponder your team reset, consider whether you need to reset your own approach. For example, has work started consuming more time and energy than is healthy? Are you taking on too much and delegating too little? This is also the perfect opportunity to consider what reset you need as the team's leader.

QUICK RECAP

Is your team feeling stuck, stymied, or a bit stale? Resetting your team can be easier than you think.

- Has your team lost sight of your purpose and goals? Focus on realignment. If your team is feeling disconnected, invalidated, or frustrated, look to revitalization.

- Realignment should be your first priority. It entails clearing up misunderstandings around your team's purpose, goals, strategies, and roles.

- Revitalization is less about *what* your team needs to do and more about *how* you do it. Focus on updating your communication habits and your team's interpersonal dynamics.

Adapted from "20 Questions to Ask When Your Team's Vibe Is Off," on hbr.org, July 19, 2023 (product #H07PT2).

Disagreement on your team?
Read this article to learn how to handle it:

Developing Your Employees

Do You Know What Motivates Your Team?

by Rik Nemanick

You may have seen it play out before: A star performer is promoted to lead a team of peers but struggles to get the most out of them. In fact, you may be (or have been) that leader. This experience is surprisingly common in organizations of all sizes and across professions. The new leader thinks, "I'll lead by example. I'll show them how hard I work and that will inspire them to work just as hard." That logic, however, is flawed.

Psychologist Daniel Goleman has referred to this style of leadership as "pacesetting."[1] It happens when the leader sets a high bar for performance and works hard (and often long hours) to raise expectations for the rest of the team. The leader runs like a pacer in a race, but runs faster than everyone else, hoping to inspire them to catch up. While a few team members can temporarily keep up, the rest slow down or push back, and the team's performance starts to deteriorate.

The gap between what the leader is trying to accomplish and what's actually achieved is often due to a mismatch in sources of motivation. The leader likely has an innate competitive drive and a strong focus on career goals. The team members probably have different motives that stem from their own ambitions, values, and individual goals, which are often different from the leader's.

As someone new to leadership, it can be easy to rely on pacesetting. You were likely promoted into your role due to your outstanding performance as an individual contributor, and now you want to hold other people to that same standard. But, as Goleman notes, pacesetting tends to erode trust and drive a wedge between managers and their teams.

When you aren't on the same page as your subordinates, several bad habits can start to sneak in. You may hesitate to delegate tasks because no one can meet your expectations. In fact, you may be tempted to take over some of your team's responsibilities since they don't have the same sense of urgency as you. You may become visibly frustrated with people and have lots of corrective feedback. You may even begin to divide important tasks and projects between the one or two team members you can trust (and who are likely the runners trying to keep pace with you).

While I don't suggest that young and ambitious leaders completely water down their high standards, if you want to get the most out of your team, it's important to recognize that each person has their own motives. Slowing down to learn those motives can help you find more effective ways to encourage each person to do their best work.

What Motivates Your Team?

Unfortunately, learning what motivates other people is not as straightforward as directly asking someone, "What motivates you?" Most of us struggle to articulate our actual motives and may not be fully conscious of them. A better approach, and one I've coached many leaders to take, involves asking three powerful questions focused on the past, the present, and the future.

Look backward: What have you accomplished?

The first question I tell my clients to ask is, "What have you accomplished in the last four to six months that makes you most proud?" I tell them to follow that question with, "What about that work makes you proud?"

The first answer gives them insight into the kind of work their team members like to do, and the second tells them what about that work makes them feel motivated.

When you ask these questions of your own team, the key is to listen for hints of intrinsic motivation—or the incentive we feel to complete a task just because we find it engaging or enjoyable. For example, if your team member answers the first question and says they're proud of writing a viral social media post simply because they really love that kind of work, they were likely intrinsically motivated by it. Now, your job is to find out why.

There are a few components that drive intrinsic motivation: competence, autonomy, and connectedness, according to self-determination theory (SDT).[2] Let's take a closer look at each:

Competence: If your team member says they find social media writing rewarding because it comes naturally to them and they find it validating when other people share their content, they may be motivated by work that makes them feel competent. SDT postulates that the satisfaction we feel when we overcome a challenge and perform well makes us feel more competent, which then leads us to feel intrinsically motivated.

Autonomy: If your team member is proud because they wrote the post in their own way without the guidance of anyone else, they likely value and are driven by the feeling of autonomy. In fact, psychologists have found that competency and autonomy often play off each other.

Connectedness: If your team member is proud because they collaborated well with others to write the post and saw it resonate widely, they may be motivated by connectedness. This means the task itself wasn't as motivating as being part of a group that accomplished it together, providing a sense of belonging.

You may hear about what accomplishing the task meant to your team member. Though this isn't included in SDT, many of us are motivated by work that is meaningful and has a purpose.

As you listen to the answers, make note of what made your team member proud (competency, autonomy, connectedness, or purpose). Start to think about what responsibilities align best with those sources of motivation. For instance, if your team member described how they worked as part of a team (connectedness) to solve an important problem (purpose), you might think about other projects you could assign them to feed these internal drives.

Look at today: What is getting in your way today?

The second question can help surface demotivators, or things that are frustrating your team and sapping their motivation. A big part of your job as a leader is to remove the barriers blocking their potential. Beyond that, this question will give your people an opportunity to feel heard and appreciated.

Some leaders are afraid to ask about barriers for fear of sur-facing things they can't change (hard deadlines or limited resources). Others worry that the conversation will devolve into a complaining session. To move past these fears, remind your-self that not every roadblock can or needs to be overcome— listening and caring can be enough. Showing empathy and being open to looking for ways to compensate for or work around a roadblock can go a long way and even help unblock your team member for the time being.

When your team member shares their frustrations, ask, "What do you think we can do about that?" (Depending on the issue, you might substitute "we" with "you" or "I.") If the issue is truly unsolvable, discuss how your team member can still be effective given the constraint. Even if the solution isn't obvious, you're still building a foundation of trust, connecting, and surfacing a frus-trating problem. You'll gain information that can help you pre-vent similar barriers in the future.

Look forward: What would you like to do more of?

The final question opens the door to what your team member would like more of going forward. There may be things they want but have never communicated to you—either because they couldn't find the right time or felt they needed permission to ask.

One team member may want to learn a new skill, while another wants to tackle a challenging project. One person may want to participate in a mentoring program, while another wants to gain experience in a different department.

As a leader, you don't have to fulfill every request, but asking the question will help you figure out how to make their jobs more interesting and motivating. It will create some room for job crafting, which involves making small changes to better fit the role to the individual.

How and When Should You Ask These Questions?

Each of these questions has the potential to yield powerful insights, but you need to be conscious of when and how you hold the conversation to see them. Here are a few tips.

Time it right

While these questions might feel like a natural fit for your annual performance evaluations, I would advise asking them sooner. The end of the year is not the time to make amends for lost motivation.

Motivating your team and helping them grow is part of your daily job. That's why I recommend asking these questions during a regularly scheduled one-on-one meeting and make them the entire focus. This will give you the space you need to have a meaningful conversation and start making changes sooner rather than later.

Give your team member a heads-up

Don't ask your team member these questions on the spot. To get the most thoughtful answers, they'll likely need some time to reflect and prepare. Consider sending the questions via email in advance of your meeting.

You might say, "In preparation for our meeting this week, I wanted you to ponder three questions. Not only will these help you reflect on your work and your future goals, but your responses will also help me plan for your growth and development."

Don't make it a onetime thing

You should be having this conversation about every six to 12 months. It's a good way to check in with your people on something besides what they are working on right now. You can also use each subsequent meeting to get feedback on any changes that have come about since your last discussion. Be sure to listen actively, take notes, and repeat back any major points your team member makes to show that you're paying attention.

The ultimate goal is to make your team members feel heard and cared for while uncovering their deepest motives. If you approach these discussions with a curious mindset and make them a regular practice, you will find them paying dividends in the form of team cohesiveness, productivity, and morale.

QUICK RECAP

To figure out what motivates your team members, ask them three powerful questions focused on the past, the present, and the future.

- **What have you accomplished that you're proud of?** Listen for hints of intrinsic motivation and think about projects you could assign them to feed those internal drives.

- **What is getting in the way today?** Surface demotivators or things that are frustrating your team. Then, try to remove the barriers blocking their potential.

- **What would you like to do more of?** Use the answer to figure out how to make their jobs more interesting and motivating going forward.

Adapted from content posted on hbr.org, October 16, 2023.

To learn more about motivating employees,
listen to this podcast:

11

How to Stop Micromanaging and Start Empowering

by Lia Garvin

As a new manager, you care. A lot. You care about your team, the work you're doing, the way you're perceived by company leaders—the list goes on.

Caring can be a good thing. But when it turns into having to control every single thing, from the wording choices in an inconsequential email to the shade of blue used in the internal team website, you've taken it to the extreme. It can be a slippery slope from kindly wanting to be looped in to full-on micromanagement.

When we think of the controlling boss, we often think of someone yelling at their employees, telling them they don't cut it, and creating an all-around hostile work environment. But this is often not the case. Micromanaging is being overly prescriptive on tasks and follow-ups—to the point of taking learning opportunities away from your team and decreasing overall team performance. Yes, your greatest weakness *can* be that you care too much.

This can be especially hard for new managers, who are working to make their mark as leaders while feeling pressure to perform well and prove themselves to their direct reports and boss. But fear not, there are ways to break the cycle.

Talk About the Outcome, Not the Process

When you ask someone to complete a task, look closely at how you frame it. For instance, if you say, "I'd like a workshop organized with [people], on [day], covering [topics], to get to [resolution]," you've figuratively and literally spelled out the whole process for someone. This level of detail and direction makes people feel like you don't trust them to figure things out, or that they're just here to follow marching orders.

Sometimes, marching orders are exactly what a task requires. But whenever possible, you should give people the autonomy and space they need to step up and be leaders. This is what great managers do—they allow people to experiment, make mistakes, learn, and grow, so that they can become stronger performers.

The next time you assign someone a task or project, talk about the outcome you want—not every step you want them to take along the way. In her book *Dare to Lead*, Brené Brown discusses the concept of "painting success." This means talking with your team about what done looks like and what a good job looks like to keep everyone on the same page.

In the example, the outcome you're looking for is the resolution. Start there. Do a detailed problem analysis, and then say to your team members, "I'm looking to achieve this outcome. How would you approach it?" Let them share. Even if you don't agree with their proposal, you've showed them that you trust them, that you're interested in their ideas, and that you value their contributions.

Set Expectations Around Feedback

If you've read to the end of the previous section, you may be thinking, "But what if my team's plan won't get me the outcome I'm looking for?"

To protect yourself from this problem, discuss when and how you'll be giving your team members constructive feedback at the start of each new project. Basically, set boundaries, but also give people space to breathe, experiment, and make mistakes within those bounds. Creativity, after all, thrives under constraints.

When you're setting expectations for how you'll give feedback, you should discuss the type of feedback you'll be sharing. Will you want to line-edit their proposal or just give directional feedback on the content? In these moments, try to stay objective and check yourself for any micromanaging tendencies.

For example, if you're eager to line-edit, ask yourself why. Who is the audience you're trying to impress? If the proposal is for an internal team meeting, do you really need to fix every slightly long sentence? Probably not. If the proposal is going out to the press or senior stakeholders, fine, open the floodgates.

Your feedback should match the consequences, and when the stakes are low and the feedback is overly detailed, it can make someone feel like they're being picked on. And when someone feels picked on, they're not in a headspace to learn.

Manage Up When Possible

Now you might be thinking, "But the work of my direct reports reflects on *me*. If it isn't perfect, it looks like I did a bad job." Not necessarily, and certainly not if you've done a good job of managing up. Your role as a people manager is to develop your people, to help them build a thriving career, and to train them to be your predecessor one day. In doing this, you have to give people the space to grow and make their own unique mark on a team.

In conversations with your own manager, talk about your team members—areas where you're helping them stretch and grow, places where they're stepping up and shining, and what your plan is for the team long term. This gives you an opportunity to show your manager "I've got this" when something isn't quite perfect.

If you feel squeezed by your manager, it's likely you'll direct some of that back to your team, even if you *really* try not to. By talking to your manager about the very same things you talk to your team members about—what success looks like on a project and when and how you'll share feedback—you have an opportunity to check (1) if they agree on your definition of success, and (2) the ways and moments they can share feedback if they'd like to chime in as well.

. . .

Managing teams is hard. It's even harder when we care. And it's even *even* harder when our team members don't do things in the exact same ways we do. But this diversity of thought is what results in growth, creativity, and innovation.

The last thing you want to do is wear someone down into working exactly like you and your own management chain. Celebrate the different ways of solving problems, of reaching successful outcomes, and create opportunities for people across your team to learn from each other. The more people feel like their ideas and ways of working are recognized and valued, the better work they do, and the longer they'll want to stay on your team.

If you're stuck in a cycle of micromanaging, it's not too late. Start right now. Let go a little bit and watch your team members rise to the occasion.

QUICK RECAP

Micromanaging can take away learning opportunities from your team and decrease overall performance. Here's how to avoid it:

- The next time you assign someone a task or project, talk about the outcome you want, not every step you want them to take along the way.

- Discuss when and how you'll be giving your team members feedback at the start of each new project, and ensure that your level of feedback matches the consequences.

- Manage up to avoid feeling squeezed by your own manager. It's likely you'll direct their micromanagement back to your team, even if you try not to.

Adapted from content posted on hbr.org,
September 9, 2022.

Worried you might be a micromanager?
Read this article:

12

A Better Way to Develop and Retain Top Talent

by Margaret Rogers

Workers with capabilities that allow them to keep up with the rapid pace of change in today's work environments—such as adaptability, technological literacy, and people management—are in steep demand. But employers are struggling to keep them on board.

One of your duties as a manager is to help develop and retain the top talent on your team. And in my experience, the most impactful development happens in small moments that occur within the workplace every day: on-the-job learning opportunities that are wholeheartedly catered to the worker's unique needs and challenges.

It might seem impossible to offer every employee this kind of personalized training, but any company can do so at scale when managers create a learning environment. Here's how.

Ask More Questions to Gain Insights on Employees

Just as a business must understand what its customers need to produce the most useful products, managers must understand what their employees need to give them ideal learning opportunities. Asking questions is the best way to do this.

Start by scheduling regular one-on-one meetings with each team member. In addition to using this time to check in on their current projects, ask them what skills they're most comfortable with and which they would like to develop. Inquire about areas that feel especially challenging.

Here are a few examples you can use to kick-start that process:

- What parts of your job are most interesting and rewarding?

- What areas are you finding most challenging right now?

- What are you doing to reach short- and long-term career goals?

- Are there any other projects, committees, or additional responsibilities you would like to be a part of?

- Is there anything else you're curious about that you haven't been able to explore yet?

In these meetings, practice active listening and try to come from a place of genuine curiosity rather than judgment. This means leaving your laptop closed and taking notes the old-fashioned way. It's also helpful to repeat what employees say during meetings in your own words to ensure you are fully understanding their insights.

Create More On-the-Job Opportunities

Once you've identified the skills your team members want to learn, look for opportunities to help people develop them. Classroom-style training is a stellar foundation, but it can lose its effectiveness if it isn't applied readily. "Learning moments" are an easier, quicker way to move the needle. These moments can be significant or small, but engaging employees in this way is key to helping them step outside their comfort zones, practice, and build confidence.

For example, imagine one of your employees is uncomfortable having tough yet necessary conversations. In a one-on-one meeting, he might express frustration about a peer whom he is struggling to collaborate with. You could take this opportunity to create a learning moment. This might be role-playing a tricky conversation or writing down a step-by-step plan of action. In this way, you are helping your team member practice and improve his communication skills in a safe setting (as opposed to simply sharing theoretical advice). The next time he comes across a similar situation, he will have tools to help him overcome it.

Treating every challenge your employees face as an opportunity for practice and growth—whether it is something personal, like improving communication skills, or practical, like learning a new technology—is critical to establishing an environment in which people believe they are valued enough as individuals to be given the time and space to flourish. It also gives managers the chance to help their employees effectively upskill and reskill on a case-by-case basis as new obstacles arise outside of formal trainings and in everyday work experiences.

Vary Learning Experiences

Consider which experiences will best cater to your direct reports' needs. Factors such as the employee's tenure, experience level, and adaptability are all variables that could impact your approach. Smaller opportunities—say, participation in projects where the employee can rely on more experienced peers for support—are best when a team member is unfamiliar with or new to a necessary skill. Bigger opportunities that require employees to take risks and stretch beyond their comfort zones are more suited to individuals who have prior experience carrying out a certain task; in these moments, they can put their skills to the test more independently and play a larger role.

Pretend, for example, you have two employees who express interest in public speaking and presentations. They both recognize it's a valuable skill to develop as they work toward becoming leaders. From previous meetings, you know one of them is less experienced than the other and is therefore more nervous about speaking in public. This employee might benefit more from a small group setting, like a lunch-and-learn during which he gives a short presentation. Because the other employee has had more practice in this area, a lunch-and-learn would not be as valuable for her. Instead, you might have her fly solo and present on a topic at the next companywide meeting or at a conference in front of a larger audience.

Save the most significant opportunities for those who are ready. These have higher stakes—for the employee, the project, and the company at large.

The level of control employees have over their growth should also vary. You might encourage a more experienced employee to design or seek out their own opportunities for growth, but a less experienced employee often requires more structure in key learning areas. Either way, it's crucial to allow employees a level of autonomy. When left alone, people will naturally find innovative ways to accomplish new things. Experimenting with autonomy also allows mistakes to be made—just as much as it allows successes to be had. This will help you identify skill gaps and brainstorm ways people can fill them.

Remember, safety is necessary when confidence is low, but pushing employees to the edge of discomfort results in real development.

Provide Regular Feedback

Feedback is perhaps the most valuable aspect of this process, and it starts with setting clear expectations. As your team continues to carry out on-the-job opportunities, work with employees to set goals to strive toward. Provide regular feedback on what they are doing well and where you see opportunities for improvement.

During this time, be patient. Reflect on the work your employee has done up to this point, making sure to discuss both successes and failures without judgment. If an employee tried something new and it didn't pan out, recognize the effort. People are more likely to grow from their experiences when they aren't punished for failure. (In fact, they're probably kicking themselves already.)

In the same vein, you can ensure employees actively apply what they've learned by putting together a plan for improvement— whether that means creating clearer deadlines, helping them better manage their time, or thinking through difficult problems when they arise. Tracking personal metrics is also a helpful way for employees to measure performance and growth on their own time.

Manage Your Time

Employee development can be overwhelming, especially when you have a large number of direct reports. Take proactive steps to avoid ending up with an unmanageable workload. Before shaping opportunities, determine how much bandwidth you have. What level of involvement and support are you capable of giving as a manager, considering everything else on your plate? Setting realistic expectations for yourself is critical.

Not all coaching has to come from you. In some cases, you may be able to distribute employee-support tasks to informal mentors, other managers, senior leaders, or peers.

. . .

When leaders try to implement these user-centered principles in their interactions, experiment with them, and continually refine their coaching based on those findings, they not only will see astounding growth but will be able to effectively engage and retain top talent. Any company can begin by making a few changes to its managerial practices. It's time for leaders to open communication channels and address each employee personally. Help your workers shape their learning and long-term contributions for the better.

QUICK RECAP

To develop and retain the top talent on your team, create an everyday learning environment.

- Ask your employees what skills they're most comfortable with and which they would like to develop.

- Treat every challenge your employees face as an opportunity for practice and growth.

- Consider which experiences will best cater to your direct reports' needs.

- Save the most significant opportunities for those who are ready, since these have higher stakes.

- Provide employees with regular feedback on what they are doing well and where you see areas for improvement.

- Set realistic expectations for what level of involvement and support you are capable of giving as a manager.

Adapted from content posted on hbr.org, January 20, 2020
(product #H05D5G).

Giving Feedback

13

You're a Leader Now. Not Everyone Is Going to Like You

by Martin G. Moore

As a manager, it's natural to want to be liked and accepted by your team. You want to win people's approval, keep them happy, and demonstrate all the desirable attributes of a great boss.

Even so, as the person in charge, almost everything you do will have the potential to trigger conflict. Consider your core responsibilities: stretching your team to reach higher standards; coaching people one-on-one; setting collective and individual goals; making tough calls; negotiating; drawing out and resolving tensions to unlock diverse thinking.

Most of these tasks will involve some form of conflict, and none of them will go hand in hand with being liked. If you're not comfortable with that, you'll struggle to do your job well and gain the respect of others.

The truth is leadership is hard. It demands that we sometimes do things that are opposite our primordial instincts. We constantly risk not being loved by the masses. It's one of the most difficult psychological barriers to overcome, but ultimately, your job is to deliver results. This means you have to make decisions that not everyone is going to like, and you can only do that if you get comfortable with conflict.

In my experience as a corporate executive and CEO in a number of different industries, I've had the opportunity to coach and mentor leaders at all levels, many of whom were able to overcome conflict aversion to become stronger, more confident leaders.

Confronting Conflict

The best place to start is with your own team. If you can master giving them one-on-one feedback—good or bad—everything else will follow.

The DNA that underpins a high-performing team is high-performing individuals. Bringing out the best in each person will require you to have countless direct, honest, and empathetic conversations. Some leaders never master this. They spend years avoiding confrontation until it's virtually impossible to ignore. This is a career killer that I've seen derail many otherwise outstanding performers.

Right now, there's probably a conversation that you're putting off, that you know deep down you need to have. If you don't want your career to flounder, stop rationalizing and avoiding. Start developing the discipline of providing your team with the feedback they need to succeed.

If you deliver your words with compassion, your team will sense that you have their best interests at heart. Being closely connected to your people in this way is a prerequisite for building trust—and if people trust and respect you, there's nothing you can't say to them. Your mutual ability to have these kinds of conversations will soon become the bedrock of your collective achievements.

The following five lenses can help you shift your mindset and find the inspiration to initiate a potentially trying chat with your team member. The next time you find yourself avoiding, consider looking through them to remind yourself why you *must* get over your fears and get on with it. This is the first step to building the trait of a great leader: a willingness to do the hard thing when it needs to be done.

Lens 1: You have a duty of care to your people

Everyone deserves competent leadership—it's a right, not a privilege. You are responsible for your people's physical and mental well-being while they're in your charge, and this is a responsibility that you shouldn't take lightly.

If you learn to put yourself in your people's shoes, your duty of care to them will outweigh your fear of giving them critical feedback. Even though it may still be daunting, you'll be more likely to push ahead.

Lens 2: You can't get results from a subpar team

The job of a leader is to build a high-performing team that delivers results, and it's impossible to build a high-performing team unless you can challenge, coach, and confront your people to bring out their best. Strong leaders put their commitment to building team capability and performance above any fear, anxiety, or discomfort they may experience. Remember this the next time you feel hesitant to offer a team member constructive criticism.

Lens 3: Your people deserve the opportunity to improve

It's heartbreaking to see how many people go through their careers without ever receiving the blindingly obvious feedback that would have made a difference. Choosing not to give constructive feedback to your people because you don't want to hurt their feelings or because you fear they will dislike you robs them of the opportunity to improve.

If someone isn't performing, that's one thing, but don't compound the felony by letting them live under the misapprehension that everything is fine if it's not. If you can muster the courage to give them the feedback they need, you'll give them an amazing gift—the opportunity to change the trajectory of their career.

Lens 4: Everyone knows the strong and weak performers

If you allow poor performance to go unchecked, you'll kill the culture. When top performers see poor performance being tolerated, they become disenchanted. Eventually, the good people leave, and mediocrity becomes the norm. Not managing individual performance marks you as a weak leader—and no one likes working for a weak leader.

Lens 5: What if you need to let them go?

Sometimes, when people choose not to meet the required standard, you have to make the tough decision to let them go. Before you go down this path, which is likely to have a significant impact on another human's life, you need to be confident that you've done everything within your power to help them. Giving feedback early and often will give you this confidence.

Respect Before Popularity

As you go into these conversations, let this be your mantra. The sooner you accept that you cannot please everyone, the better.

For every decision you make—and this includes giving tough feedback—there will be someone who thinks you should have made a different one. As a leader it is your job to listen to everyone. Give them the respect you want to receive. But, in the end, all things considered, you do what you believe is right. Although it can be disconcerting to realize that not everyone agrees, it's also strangely liberating: If you accept that you can't please everybody, it clears the path to do what you think is right, not what's popular.

Popularity doesn't matter. Doing the right thing does.

QUICK RECAP

When you find yourself avoiding giving critical feedback, look through these lenses.

- **Lens 1: You have a duty of care to your people.** This duty will outweigh your fear of delivering feedback.

- **Lens 2: You can't get results from a subpar team.** Your people can't achieve high performance unless you challenge them to do their best.

- **Lens 3: Your people deserve the opportunity to improve.** Not giving them constructive feedback robs them of the chance.

- **Lens 4: Everyone knows the strong and weak performers.** When poor performance is tolerated, mediocrity becomes the norm.

- **Lens 5: What if you need to let them go?** Be confident that you've done everything to help them first.

Adapted from content posted on hbr.org, September 16, 2021.

14

Mistakes Managers Make When Giving Feedback

by Brooke Vuckovic

Many managers view giving feedback as one of the most challenging and unpleasant parts of their jobs. Critiquing someone's performance can be an emotional, anxiety-inducing experience.

Here's the thing: No one is naturally good at giving feedback. It's a skill that's learned over time with guidance and practice. But as a manager, it's essential that you do learn it—and not just in the context of delivering yearly performance reviews. In fact, many leading companies have been dropping annual performance ratings in favor of more immediate and ongoing conversations. More than ever, real-time critiques are part of daily life for managers.

Fortunately, you can take steps to become better at providing consistent performance feedback. Start by becoming aware of the mistakes you may be making and learning what to do to avoid those pitfalls.

Mistake 1: Not Winning Trust Before Providing Feedback

A manager who gives feedback without first establishing trust is like a director who fails to set the scene before their actors take the stage. In the absence of trust, your direct reports will have a harder time hearing, accepting, and acting on your feedback.

Think about it in the context of receiving feedback from your own boss. If they seem indifferent to your career goals, provide scattered feedback without direction, and try to control your every move, are you going to readily accept and act on the feedback they provide? What about if, instead, they take the time to understand you, share feedback in the context of your aspirations, and give you space to grow and learn?

Solution

The first thing you should do as a manager is to get to know each of your team members—including their career aspirations and goals. In your one-on-one conversations, ask: "What goals are you hoping to achieve in your role over the next six months?" or "How do you see your role evolving over the next year?" Some of your direct reports may be focused on getting promoted, while others may be eager to develop skills that will help them take on higher-profile assignments.

Once context has been established, and you're clear about how you can support your team members' development, you can begin to link your feedback to their goals. For example, you might say, "I know you want to take on more responsibility, so this is an area in which you need more development. One thing you can do better is . . ." In those two sentences you go from critic to coach. Showing your direct reports that you care about their growth through your feedback will further help instill their trust in you.

Mistake 2: Avoiding or Delaying Feedback

Given the discomfort of sharing feedback with others, it's not surprising that your first instinct may be to avoid it. When you see an opportunity for giving negative feedback, for example, you may find yourself simply hoping the issue will resolve on its own. Or you may assume it will be easier to wait and deliver your feedback during a structured annual review.

But delaying feedback, or simply waiting for a situation to improve, helps no one. By avoiding these conversations, you're doing a disservice to your direct reports and the overall success of your team.

Solution

Be consistent with your feedback sessions and build them in, rather than waiting until there is an issue to address. For example, if you're giving a direct report an assignment—whether it's something brand new or with higher stakes than their usual responsibilities—add "pulse check" sessions into the calendar for the end of the assignment or when the employee completes certain milestones. If an employee is supposed to win two new accounts, you could set up pulse checks for after the first three meetings, the negotiation, and the closure stages. These scheduled debriefs should include discussing what went well and what could have been done differently (their thoughts first, and then your feedback). By engaging in this exercise, you'll establish a pattern for giving and receiving feedback in real time.

Mistake 3: Overdelivering Feedback . . . at the Wrong Time

As the saying goes, feedback is a gift. But too much can be overwhelming.

You must learn how to decide if a piece of feedback is worth giving, or if doing so would hurt the situation more than help it. This can be especially important (and difficult) when it comes to receiving and conveying feedback about your direct reports from others.

Say, for example, your team is managing a conference for your company. As the first day comes to a close, you overhear your supervisor complaining about a few elements of the event. Instead of stopping to consider if the feedback indicates a trend or just the opinion of one loud voice, you decide to deliver it to your team raw and without context. But in doing so, you alienate your team members and undermine your effectiveness as a new leader.

Solution

The solution is discernment. It's your decision whether to share the feedback you receive from others with your direct reports.

When you receive feedback for your team, remind yourself of their goals and then filter out any recommendations that won't be useful in helping them improve or reach them.

Using the prior example, let's say you received feedback that the sessions during the first day of the conference ran over the scheduled time limit. Several attendees complained about the ending feeling rushed and not being able to ask questions. That feedback, indicating a consensus of opinion among several people, will help ensure a smoother event in the future. Therefore, it would be worth conveying that feedback to your direct reports. On the other hand, if you receive feedback from one person that they didn't like the topic of a session, you may want to keep that to yourself. The random opinion of one person may not be constructive and could take your team's attention and efforts away from making impactful changes.

You also need to learn when to deliver feedback. While offering feedback promptly helps learning, there is one caveat: When emotions are running high or tanks are running low, it becomes even more important to filter and focus your feedback. For example, day one of a three-day event is *not* the time for a detailed debrief. Rather, it's a good time for focusing on one or maybe two things that might be improved the next day, like technology issues, making sure people can find the display booth, and ensuring that all speakers follow the schedule. A week later, with all the feedback from audience reactions, satisfaction survey results, and other outcomes measured, a detailed debrief will be more useful. Delaying that detailed feedback will also help to eliminate blame and give you time to brainstorm solutions together as a team.

Mistake 4: Failing to Follow Up

Even if you give feedback at the right time, use the right words, and deliver it from a place of trust, it's all useless if you don't follow up. When you give feedback without circling back, your team members could lose their motivation and may be less likely to follow through on your suggestions. Without a follow-up, you may also not realize that your team is still struggling, or the direction you suggested may not be working for them.

Solution

For feedback to work, it needs to be consistent. After providing feedback, check in with your direct reports to see how they're progressing with their development. It can be as simple as asking, "In our last check-in, we talked about you trying a different approach. How is that working for you?" When your discussions are grounded in context—connecting the dots between feedback and the person's goals and aspirations—they become supportive conversations that promote ongoing learning.

Keep in mind that feedback isn't just criticism. Positive messages demonstrate that you see your team members' efforts and reinforce trust. For example, you could say, "You've been working on refining your visual representation of customer data, and it's very noticeable! You're ready to be part of the next presentation to the division head."

. . .

Awareness of your mistakes will only get you so far—this foundational managerial skill demands repetition and practice. While it may feel uncomfortable or overwhelming at first, once mastered, it will pay dividends throughout your career.

QUICK RECAP

Providing feedback is an essential part of every manager's job to ensure high performance and development. Here are common mistakes to avoid:

- **Not winning trust before providing feedback.** Without trust, your reports will have a harder time hearing, accepting, and acting on your feedback.

- **Avoiding or delaying feedback.** Instead, be consistent with your feedback sessions.

- **Overdelivering feedback at the wrong time.** You must decide if a piece of feedback is worth giving and when, or if doing so would hurt the situation more than help it.

- **Failing to follow up.** Circle back to check in on an individuals' progress.

Adapted from "Mistakes First-Time Managers Make When Giving Feedback," on hbr.org, September 22, 2023.

How can you approach giving feedback, especially when you're dreading it? Watch this video:

Why Employees Need Both Recognition and Appreciation

by Mike Robbins

Recognition and appreciation. We often use these words inter-
changeably and think of them as the same thing. But while
they're both important, there's a big difference between them.
Leaders who want their teams to thrive and organizations that
want to create cultures of engagement, loyalty, and high performance need to understand the distinction.

Recognition is about giving positive feedback based on results
or performance. Sometimes this happens in a formal way: an
award, a bonus, a promotion, a raise. Sometimes recognition is
given more informally: a verbal thank-you, a handwritten note.
All of these methods can be meaningful, especially if they're
done in a timely and genuine way. They're also motivating and
exciting—everyone wants their good work to be applauded.

But there are some limits to recognition. First, it's performance-based, so it's conditional. Second, it's based on the past, so it's about what people have already done. Third, it's scarce. There's a limited amount of recognition to go around—everyone can't get a bonus or be mentioned by name in a memo—and it can be stressful when many people are vying for a finite amount of praise. Fourth, it generally has to come from the top. Many organizations have set up programs that allow peers to highlight each other's efforts, but the major forms of recognition (promotions, raises, and so on) are usually given by senior leaders.

And while recognition that includes monetary compensation can be great, researchers from the London School of Economics found that financial incentives can actually backfire when it comes to motivating employees. According to an analysis of 51 experiments, "these incentives may reduce an employee's natural inclination to complete a task and derive pleasure from doing so."

Appreciation, on the other hand, is about acknowledging a person's inherent value. The point isn't their accomplishments. It's their worth as a colleague and a human being.

In simple terms, recognition is about what people do; appreciation is about who they are.

This distinction matters because recognition and appreciation are given for different reasons. Even when people succeed, inevitably there will be failures and challenges along the way; depending on the project, there may not even be tangible results to point to. If you focus solely on praising positive outcomes, on *recognition*, you miss out on lots of opportunities to connect with and support your team members—to *appreciate* them.

Oprah Winfrey spoke about this in a powerful way when she gave a commencement speech at Harvard in 2013:

I have to say that the single most important lesson I learned in 25 years talking every single day to people was that there's a common denominator in our human experience. . . . The common denominator that I found in every single interview is we want to be validated. We want to be understood. I've done over 35,000 interviews in my career. And as soon as that camera shuts off, everyone always turns to me and inevitably, in their own way, asks this question: "Was that OK?" I heard it from President Bush. I heard it from President Obama. I've heard it from heroes and from housewives. I've heard it from victims and perpetrators of crimes. I even heard it from Beyoncé in all of her Beyoncé-ness. . . . [We] all want to know one thing: "Was that OK?" "Did you hear me?" "Do you see me?" "Did what I say mean anything to you?"

What Oprah was talking about is appreciation. And when we show appreciation to our colleagues, customers, managers, and partners, we're more likely to build trust and connect.

Here are a few simple ways to show appreciation for those around you:

Listen. One of the best things you can do for the people you work with is also one of the simplest: Put down your phone, turn away from your computer, and genuinely listen to them.

Tell people what you value about them. Doing this proactively—not because someone did something great or because you want something from them—is an incredibly powerful gift. It can positively affect how your colleagues feel about themselves, your relationship with them, and the culture of the team.

Check in. There's a quote I like that is often attributed to Teddy Roosevelt: "People don't care how much you know until they know how much you care." No matter who said it, it's such a great reminder. Check in with the people you work with. Genuinely asking how they're doing and what they're challenged by right now can show them that you care.

Showing appreciation for employees is especially important if you're a manager. In Glassdoor's Employee Appreciation Survey, 53% of people said feeling more appreciation from their boss would help them stay longer at their company—even though 68% said their boss already shows them enough appreciation.[1] The lesson? More is better.

Great leaders have to successfully focus on and cultivate both appreciation and recognition. And all of us benefit from understanding this distinction in business (and in life). Recognition is appropriate and necessary when it's earned and deserved. Appreciation, however, is important all the time.

QUICK RECAP

Recognition is about giving positive feedback based on results or performance. Appreciation is about acknowledging a person's inherent value. Employees need both, but you have the power to give appreciation every day. Here's how:

- **Listen.** Put down your phone, turn away from your computer, and give them your full attention.

- **Tell people what you value about them.** Doing so can positively affect how your colleagues feel about themselves, your relationship with them, and the culture of the team.

- **Check in.** Genuinely asking how your employees are doing and what they're challenged by right now can show them that you care.

Adapted from content posted on hbr.org, November 12, 2019
(product #H059FN).

Managing an Underperformer Who Thinks They're Doing Great

by Liz Kislik

When you become a manager, your hope is that everyone on your team will be a star performer. But unfortunately, that's not always the case. People underperform at work for a variety of reasons—from not understanding a project's objectives, to not feeling motivated or valued, to not having the support they need to succeed. As a leader, it's your responsibility to identify what's holding them back and help them find ways to improve.

Here are five things you can do to help underperformers move forward.

Learn More About the Underperformer

If you don't understand an underperformer's goals and interests, it will be impossible for you to determine why they're falling short in their role. Even if this person has been on your team for a while, people's motivations change as circumstances evolve. Set aside time to directly ask what's currently driving them. This is especially important if you're working in a hybrid or remote environment, where you may not have the benefit of casual, in-person contact to pick up details about family, hobbies, or past work successes.

You should also check in about their preferences regarding how they work. For example, do they prefer strict deadlines to structure their often-interrupted workdays or more flexible deadlines to help them deal with home obligations like child- or eldercare? Based on their answers, modify your management approach to match their needs. For instance, you might learn that they miss working side by side with colleagues and would perform better if they were assigned to projects that involved more regular interaction.

Revisit Your Expectations

Once you better understand the underperformer's motivations, you should also reflect on what you want most from the employee, and why you feel you're not getting it. Start by reviewing your recent directives and whether your communications about what's expected have been clear and consistent from the beginning. This

is something you do with underperformers in any context, but if you work in a remote or hybrid environment, it's even more important to ask yourself whether your statements have been ambiguous. Part of this process is separating out whether your dissatisfaction is with their work products or with the way they deliver.

If their style or approach is the problem, check to see if you're expecting them to work the way you do. If that's the case, let go of those expectations and dispassionately assess their real strengths and capacities for contributing to the team's work.

If you suspect the underperformer's difficulties come from insufficient experience, specific skill deficits, or a lack of business or organizational acumen, consider whether they need training or to partner with a more experienced colleague.

Level with Them and Be Specific

Once you better understand the underperformer (and your expectations), you need to provide direct feedback. Many people who aren't doing well have a vague feeling that something is wrong, but don't really know which of their behaviors isn't working. For example, telling a team leader that they need to be a better listener doesn't help them understand specifically what they need to do differently. It's much more helpful to explain that when they turn away during video conferences or change the subject while team members are speaking, the team loses trust and confidence in them. The feedback gives them the opportunity to actively practice modifying those behaviors.

Help Them Learn How to Improve Their Own Performance

As much as possible, use questions to encourage them to self-diagnose and to project into their own future: "How will this experience set you up to do better in the future?" I often ask coaching clients, "Why do you think I'm asking you this?" to encourage them to reach their own conclusions, rather than telling them what I have observed. Giving them an opportunity for self-discovery can provide a kind of aha moment that directly telling them your thoughts won't. This will also help you avoid micromanaging, which is a significant temptation when you're trying to be extremely clear about expectations.

Stay in Close-Enough Contact

It's on you as a manager to stay in regular touch with underperformers and to keep them in the loop. Don't assume that no news is good news. After you've given an underperformer candid feedback, if they don't hear from you, they may start to worry that you're ignoring them because you've written them off, and their performance can deteriorate further. Schedule regular meetings to talk about their progress.

If you've asked them to keep you up to date on their progress, make clear how you want them to do that. If they tend to use email, but you're awash in email and respond better to texts or Slack messages, tell them that. And don't rely only on

Firing with Compassion

by Joel Peterson

When an underperformer isn't receptive to feedback or isn't making improvements, there may come a time where you need to let that employee go. It's a difficult decision, and an even more difficult conversation. Here's how to navigate the process with fairness and empathy.

Prepare and Practice

Rehearsing for difficult conversations may be the single best way to prepare for them. Before entering a termination discussion, I engage in a series of self-talk exercises designed to reinforce the necessity of the action and put myself in the right mindset. Some of them emphasize the need to act with grace and gravitas. (*Letting this person go is one of my most important tasks. I will do it with the utmost sensitivity.*) I also remind myself that as a manager, I deserve some of the blame for the person's failure, owing to poor hiring or coaching. (*This results from my mistakes as well as theirs.*) And, to avoid becoming defensive, I focus on the optimal outcome. (*I want to help this person find a place where they can maximize their potential—a place that better fits their skills, personality, ambitions, and style of working.*)

(continued)

Deliver the Message Immediately and Clearly

When you've decided to let someone go, schedule a meeting and deliver the message within the first 30 seconds of sitting down: "We've decided to make a change/terminate your position/replace you." To drag it out—which many managers do out of discomfort at delivering painful news—invites misunderstanding and awkwardness. It also gets in the way of moving promptly to next steps—organizing the departure in a way that is most helpful to the employee and least disruptive to the organization.

Don't Overexplain the Decision

A termination meeting is a time to communicate a decision—not to debate it, defend it, or negotiate it. It's natural for people being fired to seek more information—to repeatedly ask variants of the question *Why?* You needn't offer an elaborate answer; instead, give a simple explanation for the decision—whether it's due to performance issues, needed cutbacks, or the elimination of roles or functions. If you've done a reasonable job of providing feedback, coaching, and context on the dynamics of your workplace before this conversation, the employee already has sufficient information. If the person insists on defending themselves, avoid the temptation to engage.

Be Human

Good bosses aren't automatons. They should recognize that employees who are being fired will feel an unpleasant mix of emotions. They should listen patiently to any reactions and carefully calibrate their responses. It's natural to feel sympathy or regret that you're firing someone, but expressing those emotions may encourage an attempt to leverage sympathy and debate the decision. As they deal with their own emotions, bosses must recognize the difference between empathy and compassion (which are useful in this context) and sympathy or sorrow (which can be counterproductive).

Excerpted from "Firing with Compassion," in *Harvard Business Review*, March–April 2020 (product #R2002L).

video meetings, where the lack of true eye contact can make it seem like you're getting nonverbal clues when you're not. If you're concerned that you're not getting a good read on your remote team member's state of mind, plan to have at least some of your interactions by phone and listen carefully. The tone of their voice may give you more clues about what needs intervention.

Managing underperformers isn't easy, but using specific, road-tested techniques to help them improve will strengthen not only their performance but their relationship with you as well.

QUICK RECAP

Underperformers need guidance on how they can get back on track and improve. Here are five things you can do:

- **Learn more about the underperformer.** Aim to understand their goals and interests, so you can determine why they're falling short.

- **Revisit your expectations.** Reflect on what you want from the employee, and why you feel you're not getting it.

- **Level with them and be specific.** Give them direct feedback, so they can modify their behaviors.

- **Help them learn how to improve their own performance.** Use questions to encourage them to self-diagnose and reach their own conclusions.

- **Stay in close-enough contact.** Schedule regular meetings to talk about their progress.

Adapted from "5 Tips for Managing an Underperformer—Remotely," on hbr.org, July 22, 2020 (product #H05QUZ).

Firing an underperformer can be challenging and nerve-racking. Watch this video to learn how to do it with compassion:

Managing Your Well-Being and Growth

How Leaders Can Get the Feedback They Need to Grow

by Kim Scott, Liz Fosslien, and Mollie West Duffy

When uncertainty is high, knowing where you stand—and learning about your mistakes while there's still time to fix them—is more important than ever. To be able to adapt to changing conditions and ensure that your team continues to feel supported and motivated, you need to understand what you're doing well—and where you're falling short. Soliciting clear, actionable feedback allows you to make better, more informed decisions and pivot when necessary.

Asking for feedback also creates a culture of trust and transparency. When employees feel like their input matters, they're more likely to remain loyal, engaged, and productive. They're also much more willing to surface valuable concerns and suggestions.

But uncertainty also makes it much, much harder to get honest feedback. When people feel anxious or like their jobs might be in jeopardy, they're more reticent to speak up, especially to management. Add to that the fact that when people move up the ranks in an organization, they tend to get less corrective feedback, even though a 2014 study by Jack Zenger and Joseph Folkman showed that by a three-to-one margin, people believe corrective feedback does more to improve their performance than positive feedback.[1]

In other words, right when you need it most, getting an accurate pulse on your performance as a leader becomes really, really hard. So how do you get feedback when people are least likely to offer it? How can you solicit actionable, useful advice from your reports? Neither one of you wants to have a hard conversation, but when you're the leader, it's your job to overcome that reluctance for yourself and help the other person overcome it, too.

Knowing how and when to ask for feedback is a learned skill—as is checking your (normal) defensive reaction in the face of helpful criticism (see figure 17-1). Based on our books and research, we put our heads together to outline the specific steps leaders should take to ask for feedback. The first thing to do is to ask for criticism. This is awkward at best and can be a difficult emotional journey, so here are six tips for how to successfully solicit Radical Candor from your employees.

Embrace Feeling Negative Emotions—Often

Hearing what you need to improve rarely feels good. Ask yourself: How many times each week do the people you work with tell you things that make you anxious, upset, or even defensive? How often do they tell you things that make you feel wonder-

FIGURE 17-1

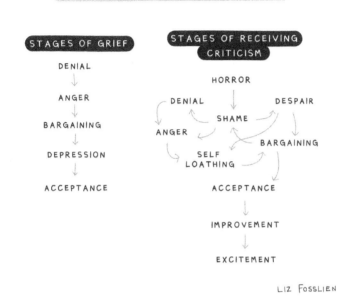

DIFFICULT EMOTIONAL JOURNEYS

LIZ FOSSLIEN

ful? If it's all feel-good praise and no hard-to-hear criticism, beware! You're not getting the real story. You need to work harder to get them to criticize you.

Remember, when it comes to soliciting Radical Candor, good news is no news, no news is bad news, and bad news is good news. As one of Liz's former managers told her, "Someone who cares about you tells you that you have food on your face. Everyone else will stay mum because they don't want to feel uncomfortable." Even though criticism is hard to hear in the moment, you need it to get better over time—and in time, it will sting less, too. (See figure 17-2.)

FIGURE 17-2

HOW IT FEELS
RIGHT NOW

HOW IT WILL FEEL
IN A FEW MONTHS

HOW IT WILL FEEL
IN A FEW YEARS

LIZ FOSSLIEN

Have a Go-To Question

It can be awkward to ask people point-blank about what's going on. And when things are uncertain, it can feel risky to them to say what they actually think. We recommend that you come up with a go-to question that establishes psychological safety. There are three elements to a good go-to question:

- The question cannot be answered with a yes or a no, or an "Oh, no, everything is fine"—which is exactly the answer you'll get most of the time if you ask, "Do you have any feedback for me?" Liz and Mollie love the question "What's one thing can I do to support you?" By asking for "one thing," you make it much more likely that you'll get a specific, actionable response.

- Your question must sound like you—something you would naturally say. The question Kim likes to use is, "What could I do or stop doing that would make it easier to work with me?" However, if those words don't fall easily off your tongue, find ones that do.

- Your question must be adapted for the person you're talking to. Jason Rosoff, who cofounded Radical Candor with Kim, told her he hates her go-to question, so she needs to ask him a more specific one.

Consider making your go-to question a recurring part of your one-on-one agendas. If your team knows what you'll be asking ahead of time, they'll have more time to prepare a useful answer.

Embrace the Other Person's Discomfort

No matter how good your go-to question is, the other person is likely to feel uncomfortable. And you're likely to feel uncomfortable because they're uncomfortable. It can be tempting to let the person off the hook at this point. But if you do that, you'll never get the feedback you need to succeed.

The only way out of this discomfort is through it. Try asking your question and then remaining silent. Count to six, slowly, in your head. Very few people can endure six full seconds of silence. They'll tell you something.

Listen to Understand, Not to Respond

When listening to feedback, your motivation matters. You should want to understand what the other person is telling you, rather than listening so that you can deliver a response. It's the difference between, "I hear what you are saying, thank you" (great) and "I hear what you are saying, but . . ." (not so great).

Feedback opens us up to seeing our behaviors from different points of view. If we're focused on defending ourselves, we lose out on the opportunity to learn and improve. A helpful hint about listening to understand: *Look* for the criticism. Often people will hide it. Sometimes you'll get Oreo feedback: two positive thoughts around a negative one. Make sure you don't miss the criticism. Other times the feedback will be more like an oatmeal raisin cookie. Don't miss the raisins! (For an illustration of types of feedback, see figure 17-3.)

Close the Loop: Make Your Listening Tangible

The best way to ensure you'll continue receiving feedback is to follow up and share the actions you've taken based on what you heard.

When you receive critical comments, it's useful to immediately outline what you'll do with the suggestions or concerns that were flagged. Try, "Here's what I'll do moving forward." And remember: You don't need to promise to make massive changes (you might not be able to deliver on those promises). You can

FIGURE 17-3

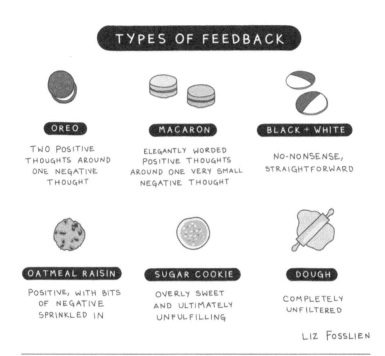

TYPES OF FEEDBACK

OREO
TWO POSITIVE THOUGHTS AROUND ONE NEGATIVE THOUGHT

MACARON
ELEGANTLY WORDED POSITIVE THOUGHTS AROUND ONE VERY SMALL NEGATIVE THOUGHT

BLACK + WHITE
NO-NONSENSE, STRAIGHTFORWARD

OATMEAL RAISIN
POSITIVE, WITH BITS OF NEGATIVE SPRINKLED IN

SUGAR COOKIE
OVERLY SWEET AND ULTIMATELY UNFULFILLING

DOUGH
COMPLETELY UNFILTERED

LIZ FOSSLIEN

say something like, "My next step will be to talk to other leaders to see what's possible."

Take former Netflix CEO and now executive chairman Reed Hastings, who receives an annual 360-degree written assessment that any employee could contribute to. Hastings closed the loop on his 2019 360 by writing a memo to all Netflix employees. Here's an excerpt from his book *No Rules Rules*:

> I find the best comments for my growth are unfortunately the most painful. So, in the spirit of 360, thank you for bravely and honestly pointing out to me: "In

meetings you can skip over topics or rush through them
when you feel impatient or determine a particular topic
on the agenda is no longer worth the time. . . . On a
similar note, watch out for letting your point-of-view
overwhelm. You can short-change the debate by signaling
alignment when it doesn't exist." So true, so sad, and so
frustrating that I still do this. I will keep working on it.

Once you've taken action, make sure you share the changes
you've made. Ask if you under- or overcorrected. Helpful hint:
If the problem is something you've struggled with for some time,
it's usually a good idea to try to overcorrect. If you get feedback
that you move too fast, work on slowing down until someone
tells you you're moving too slowly.

And if you weren't able to do anything differently, communicate why. When an employee told Kim she interrupted him
and other employees in meetings, she wore a rubber band to
her next staff meeting, told everyone about the feedback, and
asked for help in changing this deeply ingrained bad habit
that she couldn't realistically change overnight. She asked
people to snap the rubber band on her wrist when they noticed
her interrupting. (She knew that the people on her team would
actually do that, and with a laugh—you might decide to take
a different approach.) The rubber band helped her interrupt
less. But more importantly, it made her listening tangible—
and explained that although she couldn't change things overnight, she was working on it.

One of the biggest missteps we see leaders take is staying silent
when, after careful consideration, they realize they're unable to
act on feedback. When employees never hear back after giving

feedback, they'll assume that their suggestions were ignored. It's much, much better to come back to your team and say something like, "Unfortunately, due to the executive team's priorities for the quarter, we won't be able to do _____, but I'm going to keep it in mind," than to say nothing at all.

Make Giving Feedback—Not Venting— a Team Habit

Consistent venting, when you rehash the same problems without trying to understand or solve them, can make you and your team feel worse. This is because you're ingraining the frustration in your brain by talking about it over and over, without actually focusing on what can be learned or changed.

Even worse is when a person doesn't feel safe giving feedback to another person and instead vents their frustrations to a neutral third party. This may make the frustrated person feel better in the moment, but it doesn't solve anything long term, since the other person is oblivious to their frustrating behaviors. When someone comes and talks to you about someone else who is not in the room, it may feel like you're being an empathetic listener. But really all you're doing is stirring the political pot. Instead, encourage them to go talk directly with the other person. Offer your services as a mediator but remind them that it still requires both of them to talk to you at the same time. There are obvious exceptions—if a person is being bullied or harassed, don't tell them to go work it out directly.

Make feedback a team habit so that people feel safe giving it directly instead of venting to someone else. The place to start is soliciting feedback. If everyone is soliciting feedback, it's more likely to be met with open ears.

. . .

When things are up in the air, it can feel comforting to avoid difficult feedback. But creating stability for your team—and success for your organization—depends on your ability to learn what needs to change. Burying your head in the sand is never the safe thing to do. A culture of ruinous empathy or false harmony is not the path to success. Instead, invite criticism.

QUICK RECAP

Creating stability for your team depends on your ability to solicit feedback on what needs change.

- Embrace feeling negative emotions. Criticism may be hard to hear, but you need it to improve.

- Have a go-to question, such as, "What could I do or stop doing that would make it easier to work with me?"

- Embrace the other person's discomfort. After asking your question, remain silent.

- Listen to fully understand what the other person is telling you, rather than planning your response.

- Follow up on the feedback you've received and share the actions you've taken.

- Make giving feedback a team habit by encouraging individuals to speak directly to each other.

Adapted from content posted on hbr.org, March 10, 2023
(product #H07IRN).

How can you ask for and get quality feedback, react to it
(good or bad), and grow from it? Watch this video:

How Managers Can Make Time for Their Own Development

by Helen Tupper and Sarah Ellis

Being a successful manager today is a tough task that requires grappling with multiple "ands": supporting team members *and* influencing senior stakeholders; making progress on the day job *and* troubleshooting unexpected problems; delivering on quarterly objectives *and* thinking strategically. In the midst of the "and" overload, it's not surprising that managers tend to be the least likely people in an organization to prioritize their own career development.

We support thousands of managers every year who share a sense of frustration that their career development is stalling but struggle to find the time to invest in their own learning. We've observed three common career development mistakes managers make and uncovered a few tried-and-tested solutions to help them balance the demands of the day-to-day with investing in their own growth.

The Say-Do Development Gap

Our clients often tell us that they find coaching and supporting their team members' career development to be a motivating and enjoyable part of their managerial role—and yet they undervalue the importance of modeling this behavior themselves.

When teams don't see their manager investing in their own growth, it creates a say-do development gap, which has a negative ripple effect for both managers and their teams: Team members lose confidence that committing time to their professional development is the right thing to do and may even question whether their manager really values continual learning. At the same time, managers miss out on important moments to develop skills and capabilities to improve their performance and support their ambitions for the future.

What to do differently: Share learning goals

One simple and effective way for managers to avoid the say-do development gap is to share their learning goals openly with their teams. Sharing development priorities has multiple benefits. First, it prompts managers to identify what they want to focus on, and sharing their goals increases accountability. Second, involving team members means that managers are surrounding themselves with more people to support their growth and removes the idea that learning from others is linked to levels and hierarchy. Finally, when team members see their managers setting and sticking to development goals, it prompts them to do the same.

For example, a manager who shares a learning goal to increase their internal profile might benefit from a team member spotting an opportunity for them to speak at an event. A manager looking to develop their ability to use data to drive decisions could be supported with feedback from their team members on what they currently do well and what could be better.

When approached in this way, development doesn't need to be another thing that gets added to a manager's to-do list; it becomes part of their daily work and is accelerated by the people who work for them.

The Bubble Barrier

With so many demands on their workdays, it's understandable that managers rarely spend time on development outside of their organization. The challenge of finding the time and opportunity to learn in different places and with new people often feels insurmountable and falls into the category of "should do" rather than "will do."

Relying on internal-only opportunities results in managers developing a narrow view of the world and limits their learning. And operating in the bubble of internal knowledge and networks means that managers are reinforcing who and what they already know rather than cultivating their curiosity. Managers need to learn beyond the internal bubble so that it doesn't become a barrier to their growth.

What to do differently: Knowledge-swap sessions

An efficient way to bring the outside in is to approach peers in a noncompeting organization to cohost a team development session, where both teams share their expertise with each other. For example, a team with agile expertise could knowledge swap with a team that has strong communication capabilities. Or an established team in a large organization might spend time with a team from a smaller startup, exchanging insights on innovation in different operating contexts.

These knowledge-swap sessions allow everyone to spend time in a different working world, create new connections, and learn together (which also supports overcoming the say-do gap). The format of a swap session can range from a virtual hour over lunch to a full day in a meeting room. Holding knowledge swaps gives managers—and their teams—regular opportunities to learn from people outside the organization in a way that's part of their existing rhythm of work, rather than something extra to squeeze in.

The Time Trap

We often hear managers say, "I don't have time to invest in my development. I'll get around to it when everything calms down, or when this project has finished, or when I've recruited this person," and so on. This way of thinking keeps many managers stuck in a time trap, which will hold their career back over the long term.

These time traps aren't a result of managers making excuses—they reflect the reality of the challenges they're dealing with. The mistake is the hope that one day we'll magically have more time and fewer things to do. If managers look for the perfect moment to focus on their development, they're likely to be left waiting and stagnating in their career.

What to do differently: Manager micro-learning moments

Many people still associate development with formal learning methods like taking a course. But what managers need are small, easy ways to make development part of their day-to-day. Practicing micro-learning moments is a memorable and simple way for managers to kick-start the habit of continual improvement. Effective micro-learning moments usually take less than 10 minutes, and they're small but significant in their impact, as managers benefit from a compound effect of continual learning over time. Here are a few examples:

Fast feedback: Ask your team members to answer the same fast feedback question: "What three words would you use to describe me at my best?" This simple question gives managers instant insight into whether their intent is matching their impact.

One-minute weekly review: End your week by spending one minute jotting down the answers to these two self-awareness questions: What has given me the most energy this week? What could have been better this week?

Strength accelerator: Pick one skill you want to strengthen and identify an action related to regularity (how could you use that strength more?), range (where else could you use that strength that you don't today?), or reach (who could you share that strength with?).

· · ·

The more managers take control of their development, the better able they'll be to avoid the career mistakes that will get in the way of their growth. And the more their team members see the positive impact of investing in career development, the more likely they are to do the same.

QUICK RECAP

Managers tend to be the least likely people in an organization to prioritize their own professional development. How can you make time to learn and grow in your role?

- **Share your learning goals openly with your team.** This will help you stay accountable and garner support for your team members.

- **Set up knowledge-sharing sessions.** Host knowledge swaps where external groups share their expertise with your team, and vice versa.

- **Find moments for micro-learning.** Find regular time—10 minutes or less—to devote to your development, including soliciting feedback, a weekly review, or a strength accelerator exercise.

Adapted from content posted on hbr.org, June 29, 2023
(product #H07PI4).

You Don't Have to Put Yourself Last

by Nataly Kogan

Do you want to be a great leader? There is one skill you need to master that doesn't get nearly enough attention: emotional fitness.

If this is not what you expected, I'm not surprised. Every day, dozens of articles discuss how leaders must focus on improving the well-being of their teams. The popular adage of "leaders eat last" has become the standard, suggesting to many new managers that, as leaders, they need to sacrifice their well-being for that of the people they lead.

To be transparent, I bought into this advice when I was starting out in my career. For the next 15 years as a leader in technology and finance, I cared deeply about the people on my teams and prioritized their health and success over mine. I was exhausted and overwhelmed and took that as a sign that I was doing things right. I adopted the mentality that being a great leader meant being a martyr, never pausing to process my anxiety or self-doubt.

All the while, I did my best to put on a confident and positive act before my team.

But my pretending didn't work forever, and eventually, I completely burned out. I almost lost everything, including the company I had founded, my family, and my health. This was the darkest, most difficult time in my life, but it taught me a powerful leadership lesson: To be a truly impactful and caring leader, I had to put myself and my emotional fitness at the top of my priority list.

What Is Emotional Fitness?

I define emotional fitness as the skill of creating a more supportive relationship with yourself, your thoughts and feelings, and other people. The way we treat others is rooted in how we treat ourselves. That means it doesn't matter how much you care about the people you lead if you don't lead *yourself* with awareness, compassion, and a consistent investment in fueling your emotional, mental, and physical energy.

The painful reality I discovered after burning out is that I wasn't fooling my team by pretending that I was doing fine when I wasn't. Instead, I was causing them unnecessary stress and creating a culture that lacked psychological trust, which research has shown to be one of the top requirements for successful teams.

As human beings, we're great at communicating our emotions using facial expressions and body language. It's like we're all wearing an emotional whiteboard on which our feelings are displayed. Other people can see them through slightly foggy glasses: They sense how we feel but don't know exactly, and when you are in a position of power and influence, you can bet that your team is watching. If they sense that you are secretly struggling, they are going to waste time and energy trying to guess why. In my case, this led to a spiral of mistrust.

What's more, human emotions are contagious. This is particularly true within teams and between bosses and the people who report to them. Your team members can literally catch your emotions.

What Can Emotional Fitness Do for You?

If you're not already convinced that emotional fitness needs to be your number one priority, consider that it will allow you—and your team—to perform at your best. Greater well-being and happiness dramatically improve our productivity, creativity, and ability to make decisions and help others. Your well-being and emotional fitness are direct investments in you and your success.

Further, you can't teach what you don't do. You can tell the people you manage to take breaks or practice self-care, but if you don't do it yourself, they will not take your efforts seriously. When leaders carry out sustainable work practices, their team members are more engaged, have greater well-being, are more likely to stay at the organization, and have more trust. Your team will do what you do, not what you say.

How Do You Strengthen Your Emotional Fitness?

Here are three science-backed practices to begin or add to what you're already doing.

Practice emotional awareness by checking in with yourself

Get into the habit of asking yourself: "How am I feeling right now?" Do this each morning, and it will eventually become more natural to do it throughout the day.

Don't judge your answers; the purpose of this practice is simply to become aware of how you're feeling in the moment. Research shows that people who practice emotional awareness have greater well-being, because awareness gives you choices.[1] Based on how you feel, you can decide to do something to support yourself or to share a bit about your emotional whiteboard with your team, loved ones, or support system. In fact, I recommend you do so if you know you're feeling off or your energy is different from normal.

This is also a great practice to do with your team: take a few minutes during a meeting to go around and check in, asking everyone to share a few words about what's on their emotional whiteboard. This requires vulnerability and can be challenging, but by going first you give permission to everyone else to do it, too. I've witnessed teams build a greater sense of openness and connection through this exercise, which fuels everyone, including you as a leader.

Schedule mini fuel-ups throughout the day

Begin by scheduling one 15- to 20-minute break, with the goal of having at least two. Put it on your calendar and when the time comes, ask yourself: "What can I do right now to refuel and reset?" Then do it! Even a short, 10-minute walk can boost your mood, improve focus and motivation, and reduce stress.

If you only have five minutes to spare, make the best use of that time. Quality matters more than quantity, as long as what you do helps you to disconnect from your work and fuels your mental, emotional, or physical energy.

Here's a bonus idea: End your next team meeting 15 minutes early and tell everyone to spend the time doing something that fuels their energy. Ask them to report back and tell you what they did (this increases accountability), and make sure you participate.

Cultivate a daily gratitude habit

Our brains have what's called a negativity bias, which means that we are more focused on noticing what's wrong than what's good or positive. The negativity bias is useful in helping us survive (danger comes with negative stimuli), but not thrive, and constantly focusing on what's wrong and ignoring what's good depletes your energy, increases stress, and makes it difficult to gain clarity when making decisions.

The best way to counter your natural negativity bias is to practice gratitude and make it a daily habit. There is a mountain of studies that show how gratitude improves well-being and resilience.

My favorite practice is called the "morning gratitude lens": Before you grab your phone, read the news, or check social media or email in the morning, pause and think of three things you're grateful for. Be specific and zoom in on small things: "I am grateful for having a few minutes to drink my coffee this morning" is better than "I am grateful for my health." Specificity helps your brain pause and really feel the gratitude. Jot down what you are grateful for in a journal, on a Post-it Note, or in the Notes app on your phone.

I also encourage you to become more intentional about expressing your gratitude to people you manage. Being on the receiving end of gratitude doesn't just feel good, but also increases motivation and engagement, and can build a stronger sense of connection and trust within a team.

Remember: You can't give what you don't have.

This is the advice I would give to my younger self. If you want to be a great leader, which means you want to positively impact other people's capacity to thrive, you have to begin by positively impacting your own capacity to thrive. Practicing your emotional fitness skills of awareness, energy management, and gratitude is a great way to start.

QUICK RECAP

To be a great leader, you need to master the skill of emotional fitness.

- Get into the habit of asking yourself: "How am I feeling right now?" Based on how you feel, you can decide to do something to support yourself or to share how you're feeling with your team, loved ones, or support system.

- Schedule at least one 15- to 20-minute break every day. When the time comes, ask yourself: "What can I do right now to refuel and reset?" Then do it.

- Cultivate a daily gratitude habit to improve your well-being and resilience. Pause and think of three specific things you're grateful for.

Adapted from content posted on hbr.org,
January 24, 2022.

For more on self-awareness as a leader,
listen to this podcast:

NOTES

Chapter 3

1. Courtney Connley, "Why Black Workers Still Face a Promotion and Wage Gap That's Costing the Economy Trillions," CNBC, April 16, 2021, https://www.cnbc.com/2021/04/16/black-workers-face-promotion-and-wage-gaps-that-cost-the-economy-trillions.html.

2. Cathy Melocik, "The Concrete Wall," Tuck School of Business, January 26, 2022, https://www.tuck.dartmouth.edu/news/articles/the-concrete-wall.

3. "Community & Belonging," Stanford Residential Education, n.d., https://resed.stanford.edu/neighborhoods/neighborhood-concept/core-principles/community-belonging.

Chapter 4

1. Nela Richardson and Marie Antonello, "People at Work 2023: A Global Workforce View," ADP Research Institute, 2023, https://www.adp.com/-/media/adp/resourcehub/pdf/adpri/global-workforce-trends-insight.pdf.

2. Amy C. Edmondson, "Psychological Safety," https://amycedmondson.com/psychological-safety/.

Chapter 6

1. Ethel Brundin, Feng Liu, and Thomas Cyron, "Emotion in Strategic Management: A Review and Future Research Agenda," *Long Range Planning* 55, no. 4 (2022).

Chapter 7

1. Chang Chen, "Shocking Meeting Statistics in 2021 That Will Take You by Surprise," Otter.ai, December 24, 2020, https://otter.ai/blog/meeting-statistics.

2. John Rampton, "The Psychological Price of Meetings," *Calendar* (blog), May 7, 2019, https://www.calendar.com/blog/the-psychological-price-of-meetings/.

3. Lebene Richmond Soga et al., "Unmasking the Other Face of Flexible Working Practices: A Systemic Literature Review," *Journal of Business Research* 142 (March 2022): 648–662.

4. Soga et al., "Unmasking the Other Face of Flexible Working Practices."
5. Tim Jacks, "Research on Remote Work in the Era of Covid-19," *Journal of Global Information Technology Management* 24, no. 2 (2021): 93–97.
6. Benjamin Laker et al., "How Job Crafting Can Make Work More Satisfying," *MIT Sloan Management Review*, September 17, 2020, https://sloanreview.mit.edu/article/how-job-crafting-can-make-work-more-satisfying/.

Chapter 8

1. Daan van Rossum, "What Hybrid and Remote Employees Really Want," FlexOS, October 20, 2023, https://www.flexos.work/learn/research-report-what-hybrid-and-remote-employees-really-want.
2. Panos Photopoulos et al., "Remote and In-Person Learning: Utility Versus Social Experience," *Springer Nature Computer Science* 4, no. 2 (2023): 116.

Chapter 10

1. Daniel Goleman, "Leadership That Gets Results," *Harvard Business Review*, March–April 2000, https://hbr.org/2000/03/leadership-that-gets-results.
2. Richard M. Ryan and Edward L. Deci, "Self-Determination Theory and the Facilitation of Intrinsic Motivation, Social Development, and Well-Being," *American Psychologist* 55, no. 1 (January 2000): 68–78.

Chapter 15

1. Glassdoor Team, "Employers to Retain Half of Their Employees Longer If Bosses Showed More Appreciation," Glassdoor Survey, November 13, 2013, https://www.glassdoor.com/employers/blog/employers-to-retain-half-of-their-employees-longer-if-bosses-showed-more-appreciation-glassdoor-survey/.

Chapter 17

1. Jack Zenger and Joseph Folkman, "Your Employees Want the Negative Feedback You Hate to Give," hbr.org, January 15, 2014, https://hbr.org/2014/01/your-employees-want-the-negative-feedback-you-hate-to-give.

Chapter 19

1. Cortland J. Dahl, Christine D. Wilson-Mendenhall, and Richard J. Davidson, "The Plasticity of Well-Being: A Training-Based Framework for the Cultivation of Human Flourishing," *PNAS* 117, no. 51 (December 7, 2020): 32197–32206, https://www.pnas.org/doi/10.1073/pnas.2014859117.

INDEX

ABOUT THE CONTRIBUTORS

RON CARUCCI is a cofounder and managing partner at Navalent, working with CEOs and executives pursuing transformational change. He is the bestselling author of eight books, including *To Be Honest* and *Rising to Power*.

JENNIFER DARY is a leadership coach and the founder of Plucky. In the past decade, she has worked with hundreds of tech leaders, is a frequent podcast guest, and travels widely to teach professional workshops. She lives in Arlington, Virginia, with her husband and sons.

LIANE DAVEY is a team effectiveness adviser and professional speaker. She is the author of *The Good Fight* and *You First* and the coauthor of *Leadership Solutions*.

MOLLIE WEST DUFFY is the coauthor of the *Wall Street Journal* bestseller *No Hard Feelings: The Secret Power of Embracing Emotions at Work* and *Big Feelings: How to Be Okay When Things Are Not Okay*. She is the head of learning and development at Lattice and was an organizational design lead at global innovation firm IDEO. She has worked with companies of all sizes on organizational development, leadership development, and workplace culture.

SARAH ELLIS is the cofounder of Amazing If, a company with a mission to make careers better for everyone. Together with her business partner, Helen Tupper, she is the coauthor of two *Sunday Times* bestselling books, *The Squiggly Career* and *You Coach You*. Sarah and Helen are also the hosts of the podcast *Squiggly Careers*, which has had 4 million downloads, and their TED Talk, "The Best Career Isn't Always a Straight Line," has been watched by almost 2 million people.

LIZ FOSSLIEN is the coauthor and illustrator of the *Wall Street Journal* bestseller *No Hard Feelings: The Secret Power of Embracing Emotions at Work* and *Big Feelings: How to Be Okay When Things Are Not Okay*. She is on the leadership team of Atlassian's Team Anywhere, where she helps distributed teams advance how they collaborate. Liz regularly leads workshops for leaders; her clients include Google, Paramount, and the US Air Force. Liz's writing and work have been featured by TED, the *Economist*, *Good Morning America*, the *New York Times*, and NPR.

LIA GARVIN, the "Team Whisperer," is a team operations consultant helping team leaders and small-business owners find ease in managing people and simplifying the way work gets done on their teams. She is the author of two bestselling books, *The Unstoppable Team* and *Unstuck*; the host of the *Managing Made Simple* podcast; a TEDx speaker; and a former team operations leader at Google, Apple, and Microsoft. Learn more at liagarvin.com

JODI GLICKMAN is a keynote speaker and the CEO of leadership development firm Great on the Job. She is the author of *Great on the Job* and a contributor to the *HBR Guide to Networking*.

CLAIRE HUGHES JOHNSON is a corporate officer and adviser for Stripe, a global technology company that builds economic infrastructure for the internet. Prior to Stripe, Claire spent 10 years at Google leading a number of business teams. She is the author of *Scaling People*.

LIZ KISLIK helps organizations from the *Fortune* 500 to national nonprofits and family-run businesses solve their thorniest problems. She is the creator of BetterAtWorkWithLiz.com, an animated miniseries about resolving difficult workplace situations. She has taught at NYU and Hofstra University, and has a popular TEDx Talk, "Why There's So Much Conflict at Work and What You Can Do to Fix It."

NATALY KOGAN is a leading expert on emotional fitness and leadership and a sought-after international keynote speaker who has appeared in hundreds of media outlets, including being profiled in the *Wall Street Journal.* Her work has also been featured in the *New York Times, Inc., Fast Company, Harvard Business Review, Time*, and others. She is the founder of Happier, Inc., and has worked with hundreds of top companies, teams, and leaders through her Happier@Work and leadership programs. Nataly is the bestselling author of *Happier Now* and *The Awesome Human Project*. She also hosts *The Awesome Human Podcast* that people call their "best-self hour."

BENJAMIN LAKER is a professor of leadership at Henley Business School, University of Reading.

KELA LESTER is a strategist who scales brands through fun, process, and innovation. See her work at thejalex.com.

ASHISH MALIK is a professor of human resources management at the Queen's University of Belfast, Northern Ireland, UK.

MARTIN G. MOORE is the author of *No Bullsh!t Leadership* and the host of the *No Bullsh!t Leadership* podcast. He cofounded his business, Your CEO Mentor, with his daughter, Emma Green. Their purpose is to improve the quality of leaders globally through practical, real-world leadership content. For more information, visit martingmoore.com.

RIK NEMANICK is a consultant specializing in leadership development. For over 20 years, he has worked with organizations of all sizes to develop their leadership talent. He is an ICF Professional Certified Coach and has coached hundreds of leaders to improve their effectiveness. In addition to his consulting, Rik is adjunct faculty in the Olin School of Business at Washington University in St. Louis.

VIJAY PEREIRA is a distinguished professor of strategic and international human capital management at NEOMA Business School.

JOEL PETERSON is the Robert L. Joss Adjunct Professor of Management at Stanford University's Graduate School of Business, where he has taught for more than 30 years. He is also the former chairman of JetBlue and the author of *Entrepreneurial Leadership*.

AMANDA REILL is an author, speaker, coach, and executive ghostwriter. She offers executive consulting services to organizations and individuals worldwide.

MIKE ROBBINS is the author of five books, including his latest, *We're All in This Together*. He is a sought-after speaker and consultant who has worked with leaders, teams, and *Fortune* 500 companies for two decades. Learn more at Mike-Robbins.com.

STEVEN G. ROGELBERG is the Chancellor's Professor at the University of North Carolina at Charlotte for distinguished national, international, and interdisciplinary contributions. He is the author of *Glad We Met*. He writes and speaks about leadership, teams, meetings, and engagement. Find more information at stevenrogelberg.com.

MARGARET ROGERS is the chief executive officer at Pariveda Solutions, a consulting firm specializing in business, brand, and technology. She holds the belief that purpose and profit can coexist, fostering the development of superior business models. To achieve this, she employs user-centered methods to lead high-performing teams. Prior to Pariveda, she led multifunctional teams serving clients across various industries within strategy, product development, and management.

KIM SCOTT is the author of *New York Times* and *Wall Street Journal* bestsellers *Radical Candor* and *Just Work* and the co-founder of the company Radical Candor. Kim was a CEO coach at Dropbox, Qualtrics, Twitter, and other tech companies. She was a member of the faculty at Apple University and previously led AdSense, YouTube, and DoubleClick teams at Google. Before that Kim managed a pediatric clinic in Kosovo and started a diamond-cutting factory in Moscow. She lives with her family in Silicon Valley.

RAMONA SHAW is a professional leadership coach, trainer, author, and podcast host. Her company Archova helps first-time and advancing managers develop the competencies required in their new roles so that they can become confident and effective leaders that people love to work for. Learn more about her work and find free tools for managers at archova.org.

LEBENE SOGA is a professor of entrepreneurship and management practice at Leeds Business School, Leeds Beckett University, UK.

GLEB TSIPURSKY, PHD, was lauded as "Office Whisperer" and "Hybrid Expert" by the *New York Times* for helping leaders use hybrid work to improve retention and productivity while cutting costs. He serves as the CEO of the future-of-work consultancy Disaster Avoidance Experts. He has written seven bestselling books, including *Returning to the Office and Leading Hybrid and Remote Teams*. His expertise comes from over 20 years of consulting for *Fortune* 500 companies, from Aflac to Xerox, and over 15 years in academia as a behavioral scientist at University of North Carolina at Chapel Hill and Ohio State.

HELEN TUPPER is the cofounder and CEO of Amazing If, a company with an ambition to make careers better for everyone. Together with her business partner, Sarah Ellis, she is the coauthor of two *Sunday Times* bestsellers, *The Squiggly Career* and *You Coach You*. Sarah and Helen are also the hosts of the podcast *Squiggly Careers*, which has had 4 million downloads, and their TED Talk, "The Best Career Isn't Always a Straight Line," has been watched by almost 2 million people.

BROOKE VUCKOVIC is a clinical professor of leadership at the Kellogg School of Management, where she teaches on a wide variety of leadership topics, including the moral complexity in leadership. Brooke received Kellogg's most prestigious teaching award, the L. G. Lavengood Professor of the Year, in 2021.

Accelerate your career with HBR's Work Smart Series.

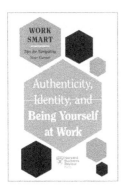

If you enjoyed this book and want more career advice from *Harvard Business Review*, turn to other books in **HBR's Work Smart Series**. Each title explores the topics that matter most to you as you start out in your career: being yourself at work, collaborating with (sometimes difficult) colleagues, maintaining your mental health, and more. **HBR's Work Smart Series** books are your go-to guides to step into and move forward successfully in your professional world.